The Journey Itself

For Alison + Jeff
B. J. Brechin

BARBARA STREET BRECHIN

outskirtspress
DENVER, COLORADO

The opinions expressed in this manuscript are solely the opinions of the author and do not represent the opinions or thoughts of the publisher. The author has represented and warranted full ownership and/or legal right to publish all the materials in this book.

The Journey Itself
All Rights Reserved.
Copyright © 2014 Barbara Street Brechin
v3.0

Cover Photo © 2014 JupiterImages Corporation. All rights reserved - used with permission.

This book may not be reproduced, transmitted, or stored in whole or in part by any means, including graphic, electronic, or mechanical without the express written consent of the publisher except in the case of brief quotations embodied in critical articles and reviews.

Outskirts Press, Inc.
http://www.outskirtspress.com

ISBN: 978-1-4787-0160-6

Outskirts Press and the "OP" logo are trademarks belonging to Outskirts Press, Inc.

PRINTED IN THE UNITED STATES OF AMERICA

Table of Contents

The Klondike and Canada's Northwest Territories • 1

Himalayan Kingdom of Tibet • 11

Millionaire Homestays in Bombay • 22

Pony Trek in the Himalayas • 30

Antarctic Adventure: Sailing to the Bottom of the World • 58

Wild Exotic Papua New Guinea • 77

The Elusive Northwest Passage • 86

Seeking His Holiness the Dalai Lama • 99

Camel Safari in Rajasthan • 116

Circumnavigating the World • 142

Prologue

The Author Speaks

Many years ago I came across a definition for travel: "Travel is a dream, an education, an experience. It's an escape from the work-a-day routine to an exciting world of different cultures, customs and attitudes. Happy is the person who turns that dream into reality."

Anonymous

It has been my good fortune to have realized that dream. I have often asked myself this question: "When was it that I began to dream of such amazing experiences?" Subconsciously it might have been in public school when I memorized Robert Louis Stevenson's poem "Travel." Many years have passed and sadly, I cannot recite it today.

However, a few years ago I was surprised to discover that I had been to many of the places mentioned in the poem. Another factor could have been my grade five social studies course. Based on the book *Pirates and Pathfinders*, we learned about the adventures of Marco Polo, Magellan, Francis Drake, Captain Cook, Scott, Amundsen, Franklin, and many others. They had captured my imagination as a ten-year-old, and much later when I taught this course.

Or it might have been the influence of the stories told to me by Lt. Col. R.C. Phelps. My Uncle Roy, who spent 30 years in Burma and India, spoke of the magnificent Taj Mahal, the Paradise on Earth that is the Vale of Kashmir, in the foothills of the Himalayas--my favorite destination in the world...until I went to Tahiti. Whatever the cause, with my first trips--Trans Canada to Vancouver, in '72, Trans Atlantic on the QE2 in '73, and numerous visits to the Caribbean and Mexico--I soon realized that I was hooked...addicted to travel, if you will!

Each summer, from 1980 on, I went on what my children called "Mom's Big Trip." Thus the dream was beginning to be realized. Places began to, as I jokingly used to say, "call me." Fellow travelers would sit with me at hotels in far-off places as we talked of where we'd been and where we still hoped to go. I began to create a travel wish list. If you could view my slides you would be looking at places that were once on that list. Only one major trip still eludes me: the Trans Siberian Rail Journey from Moscow to Beijing, with a side trip into Mongolia and a camp-out in the Gobi Desert, in a yurt! That trip, which I had booked in 1985, was canceled and I had to settle for Tibet. Thank goodness I did, as the visit to Tibet, in some ways, changed my life.

Still on the list are: Egypt, Victoria Falls, the North Pole .... There really can be no end of wishing, for one addicted to travel. Something I wrote in my "Nothing Book"--a book of my favorite poems, and ones I have written myself--gives evidence of this.

>New horizons!
>May they ever appear to me; beckon me; elude me,
>By their ever-receding distance from my immediate grasp.
>For my hope is to never satisfy the desire to continue the journey.

Barbara Street Brechin © 1990

The desire will always be there, but I must acknowledge certain factors that might prevent me from actually taking more of these trips: terrorism, war…my age. Let's not dwell on the last one! The Klondike story is the first of many trips which I took from 1980 to 2000. Not all of the thirty or more trips will be in this book, particularly those which a venturesome traveler would consider to be rather mundane.

I did organize a travel company, which I named Connoisseur Travelplan Enterprises, Inc. I picked trips that wholesalers had already planned, sought out tour members, and went on the trip as their guide--not that I would be able to know everything about the said trip. Local guides did all of that. I was in charge of flights, hotels, etc. and making sure that my group was having a good time. My first Connoisseur journey was to China, with 22 people. I chose Cultural Tours, in Vancouver, for that one and jokingly say, "It was a huge success, as no tour members were lost!"

However, the stories in this book are not ones planned by Connoisseur. So allow me to return to the first adventureseome trip that I took on my own. The Klondike trip will reveal my favorite Canadian travel experience: a cruise up the inside passage from Vancouver to Juneau and Skagway, Alaska. At Skagway, with our disembarkation we would begin a rail journey on the very old train known as The White Pass and Yukon Railway. That journey would take us to Whitehorse and Dawson City; then it would be up the Dempster Highway by bus to Inuvik and Tuktoyaktuk. It has been said that destinations such as Alaska, the Yukon, and the Northwest Territories appeal to people with a sense of adventure, enthusiasm for life, and a love of the great outdoors. I am convinced that this is true.

I believe other factors may have been at play here. You should know that my Grandfather, Milo G. Phelps, had a brother in

Whitehorse. Willard Leroy "Deacon" Phelps had travelled to the Yukon in 1898 at the time of the gold rush. However, most of the best claims were already made in 1886 and 1887, so he had missed the best of it. Not to worry. Willard (my grandfather's brother) was a lawyer, and there was plenty of work for him to do. So, with this in my background, my desire to seek out one of the world's last frontiers was preordained. Grandpa Phelps' diary, written in 1932, recounted his experiences in this part of Canada. I hoped to discover similar experiences and more, as I was off on my first big trip--alone!

The Klondike and Canada's Northwest Territories

Our Princess Cruise ship sailed from Vancouver to Juneau, Alaska where I saw my first glacier, and even walked on it. I can imagine that this Mendenhall Glacier has receded significantly in the past 33 years, as have so many other glaciers. At Skagway, Alaska we were about to experience a great thrill as we boarded the very old White Pass and Yukon Railway, which would take us over the White Pass and into the remote wilderness of Bennett Lake and the city of Whitehorse. If you get a chance, look it up on YouTube. You will see what I saw all those years ago. Built in 1900, this narrow-gauge railway was driven through the coastal mountains to connect Skagway, Alaska with Whitehorse in the Yukon. The new link made unnecessary the grueling journey over the legendary Chilkoot Pass and the crossing of Bennett Lake, to reach the Yukon River. Now that I am better-informed about the history of the White Pass and Yukon railway, I regret my words on first sight of Old Engine #73. "You must be kidding. Surely we are not going to ride on that!" How gauche of me to demean this train, when I knew nothing of its amazing history.

Minutes later, we were comfortably seated in easy chairs, which all faced the windows on the other side. Obviously this was to afford the passengers a great view of what lay ahead. It soon became apparent to me that I would be unable to photograph the unbelievably picturesque scenery seated in the old parlor car—so, undaunted by a sign that stated, "No passengers allowed," I chose to spend the rest of the trip on the platform between the rail cars, with my feet braced against the grillwork.

The rewards were well worth the risk. We gazed into deep gorges, up at rugged mountain peaks and across sparkling mountain lakes. We wound our way through dark tunnels, crawled across narrow bridges, and snaked along beside the old Klondike trail of '98. Names that conjure up excitement and drama marked our journey: Pitchfork Falls, Black Cross Rock--where a black cross marks the resting place of two men buried alive with the blasting of a 100 ton rock, in 1898; Bridal Veil Falls--where as many as 22 cataracts have been seen tumbling down the gorge; Chilkoot Pass--entranceway to the territory whose nearly vertical cliff tested the steely determination of stampeders who were required to climb and reclimb its icy steps laden with portions of the 1760 pounds of supplies demanded by the Canadian Mounties for admittance to the territory.

From Tunnel Mountain, 1000 feet above the floor of the gulch, I was afforded, to say the least, a remarkable view! The wobbly trestle swayed in the wind, but from my precarious vantage point I was able to see the train's caboose from the steepest non-guarded railway in the world. At Inspiration Point we could look south to the upper reaches of the Lynn Canal. A monument at this summit records an incident that occurred during the Gold Rush of '98. 3000 horses fell to their death in the canyon below, in what came to be known as Dead Horse Gulch.

We stopped at White Pass Summit--elevation 2900 feet--and cleared US customs. The Fraser Lake district, at the headwaters of the Yukon River, marked our entry into Canada. Beaver Lake, Lake Lindeman, and Lake Bennett followed. In 1898,

The Klondike and Canada's Northwest Territories

over 10,000 stampeders paused at Lake Bennett to build rafts and crude boats to transport themselves and their equipment through Bennett, Tagish, and Marsh Lakes to the Yukon River.

Our grub stop at Bennett Lake provided us with a typical Gold Rush meal, served Klondike style: caribou, baked beans, and home made apple pie were devoured by a very hungry group of tourists. It was here, at Bennett Lake, that I was able to capture, on film, what it means to be a proud Canadian. Because my travel history was practically nil at that time, I deemed that there must be few places on earth that could match this part of Canada in its exquisite beauty. Bennett Lake appeared as a deep turquoise-blue jewel set amidst the mauves and grays of surrounding mountains, bordered with rich green evergreen forests. "Ah yes," I whispered, "The true north, strong and free--and oh so beautiful!"

Carcross, at the north end of Lake Bennett, is a fascinating Yukon town. Great herds of caribou once crossed here by means of a natural ford--hence the name Caribou Crossing (Carcross). My Great-uncle Willard spent his summers here at what was called a cabin. I believe it to have been a very elaborate building, as described by my Grandfather Phelps when he met his brother Willard here on June 24,1932. From my grandfather's diary, the following entry seems pertinent. "We all went over to Willard's log cabin. It is a big place with lots of room inside. All kinds of bear, sheep, and other animal rugs are on the floor; deer, moose, and owls adorn the walls. A Japanese maid serves wonderful meals. Yes, it's a grand place to spend the summer."

Stampeders reached the mighty Yukon River from Bennett Lake once the ice went out in the spring. But the Yukon River System, one of the ten largest waterways in the world (2300 miles long and emptying into the Beaufort Sea), is difficult to navigate. Travelers soon ran into the treacherous section of Miles Canyon that provided only a narrow passageway and threw in tricky whirlpools for good measure. Those who made it through this challenge were met with yet another surprise: the Whitehorse Rapids. By May 29, 1898 a total of 7124 craft of every shape, size, and description had left Bennett Lake. More than a hundred were wrecked at the canyon and rapids. Today, the rapids are marked by the city of Whitehorse, Yukon's capital. Although Whitehorse provides little for tourists to do in the winter, in summertime activities abound.

My visit included a boat cruise through Miles Canyon. What had once been a hair-raising journey has now become a leisurely cruise. We sailed aboard M.V. Schwatka, a vessel that had been purchased by another of my relatives who was still living in Whitehorse in 1980 when I was there. John Scott's daughter was married to Willard's son, I believe.

We were able to enjoy numerous meals at a number of the restaurants in Whitehorse. We had our pick of Mexican, Greek, Chinese, Italian, French, and Austrian. However, I usually chose typical Yukon cuisine. After all, how often would this be a choice? My first dinner there was fantastic. The menu offered Alaska King crab or salmon, Pacific halibut, porterhouse steak, Caesar salad, wonderful pastries, and other fabulous desserts.

Our group attended the Frantic Follies Vaudeville Revue, which brought to life the true Klondike themes. I was particularly entertained by the high-kicking can-can dancers and the recitation of one of Robert Service's poems, which I had studied at school. The "Cremation of Sam McGee" was delightfully presented by the Frantic Folly players. The following day we passed Lake Le Barge on our way to Dawson City by bus. I wondered if it really was true that "On the marge of Lake Le Barge they cremated

Sam McGee." To give you a taste of the bard's work, I give you some of the lines of his famous Klondike poem.

> "I do not know how long in the snow I wrestled with grisly fear;
> But the stars came out and they danced about
> Ere again I ventured near.
> I was sick with dread, but I bravely said: "I'll just take a peep inside.
> I guess he's cooked, and it's time I looked."
> Then the door I opened wide.
> And there sat Sam, looking cool and calm, in the heart of the furnace roar;
> And he wore a smile you could see a mile,
> And he said : "Please close that door.
> It's fine in here, but I greatly fear
> You'll let in the cold and storm --
> Since I left Plumtree, down in Tennessee,
> It's the first time I've been warm."

Robert Service

Dawson City, former capital of the Yukon, became a boom town during the gold rush. The population grew to 30,000 and featured Diamond Tooth Gertie's gambling casino among many other places of entertainment. Diamond Tooth Gertie was the name assigned to the most popular dancer. Allegedly she had made a space between her front teeth to insert a diamond. She hoped it would add to her fame and popularity with the miners who had struck gold. Diamond Tooth Gertie's is Canada's oldest gambling hall, and I understand that it still exists today, in 2013. Tourists can enjoy a beverage while playing: blackjack, roulette, Texas Hold'em, poker, and the inveterate slot machines. I tried blackjack, but didn't win anything.

The Journey Itself

They are still looking for gold "in them thar hills," but the process now uses hydraulic equipment. Some old-timers may resort to their old ways. The tour operator gave us an opportunity to try panning for gold, old-style. However, I sensed that the stream we were taken to had been seeded with some fine bits of gold, as everyone found about a thimbleful. I had mine put into a locket. Although the gold rush was over less than 10 years after it began, more than $96 million in gold had been mined from the Klondike Valley. Despite this, very few miners became millionaires, and most stampeders were unable to find the elusive gold nuggets or precious gold dust. They went home, or north to Alaska, where gold strikes had been made near Nome.

Some say that there is as much gold in the tailings as was ever acquired at the time of the gold rush. Others believe in the myth of the Klondike mother lode, a source located somewhere above the creeks. Prospectors still follow the dream--among them one of my relatives, John Scott, who was then in his late seventies.

From Dawson City we cruised the Yukon River aboard the Yukon Lou. The highlight of this day was to be a salmon bake on the shores of the Yukon. We watched as they cleaned some of the big ones that didn't get away--28 pounds and more. I had my picture taken with some of these big fish, but I didn't catch any myself. At that time, the largest fish ever taken from the Yukon River weighed 118 pounds. Now, in my book, that would have been a whopper! On Paradise Island I had the best salmon I had ever tasted, baked over open coals and done to perfection. The freshly baked sourdough biscuits, baked potatoes, veggies, and homemade chocolate layer cake that accompanied the salmon made a perfect Klondike meal.

Next on our road to adventure was the Dempster Highway, another name for the newly completed Arctic Highway. It had just been completed in 1979 and cuts across mountain ranges, rivers,

The Klondike and Canada's Northwest Territories

and the Arctic Circle as it makes its way to Eagle Plains--364 miles from Dawson City and 726 miles to Inuvik on the Beaufort Sea. Since there is literally no place on the Dempster where fuel or bus repairs can be obtained, until you reach Eagle Plains, we had a C.B. on board; mandatory notification had been given to the Mounties that we were travelling the highway; and our driver had extra distributor caps and parts for the bus. As well, we had extra food and water. For part of its route, the Dempster follows the path used by the dog sled patrols of the Northwest Mounted Police, in the first half of the 20th century. Beginning in 1905, for over 25 years, patrols set out from Dawson City on their 500-mile journey to the Mackenzie River Delta. They visited Indian encampments and carried mail to settlements in the northwest. In all of those years, the only tragedy was the loss of the Fitzgerald Patrol in 1911.

Spectacular is the only word that effectively describes the first half of the views one sees on this highway, which crosses the Ogilvie Mountains, a northern extension of the Rockies. Our bus wound its way through stands of dark-green spruce and contrasting light-green poplar. Fortunately, we had perfect weather for our trip. The hard dirt road, in the bright sunlight, was quite a different thing than some travelers had previously experienced. Rain and muddy driving conditions on some of the previous trips, of which there had only been four before mine in 1980, had necessitated an urgent call to the Mounties and the assistance of a heavy road grader to haul the bus up some of the hills.

We passed Tombstone Mountain (7000 feet), set among rolling hills, Arctic tundra, and meadows of hot pink fireweed; then the typically rounded limestone mountains at Windy Pass (2300 feet) and the Hart Mountain migration route, which the caribou follow in mid-October. Next we began the climb to Eagle Plains, where we would spend the night. We stopped to take pictures at several points, and I got some amazing shots. However, neither

The Journey Itself

the photos nor any of my words can adequately describe the beauty of these places. In the distance, like a painted backdrop for some Hollywood movie, the soft blue-grays changed moment by moment as the sun began to set. Below me, in the nearer distance, were the rolling grey-green plains. At my feet, the gorgeous pink fireweed--floral emblem of the North West Territories--and all about me tall, dark-green spruce trees.

On the night of August 3, we sat in the lounge of the newly opened million dollar Eagle Plains Hotel and watched the sun drop below the horizon. As you may know, in the high Arctic in August, the sun barely sets. It disappeared at 11.40 p.m. and rose again at 1:00 a.m. Had we been there from early June to July we would not have seen the sunset at all, as there are 24 hours of daylight at that time.

I am often asked, "In all of your travels, which was your favorite destination?" Until I went to Tahiti, the top three had always been: Kashmir, in the foothills of the Himalayas; the Potala Palace in Lhasa, on the Roof of the World, in Tibet; and Eagle Plains, in the Northwest Territories of Canada. I could never pick just one. However, now that I have been to Tahiti and seen many of their glorious islands, I must add a fourth--Bora Bora, in particular.

We crossed the Arctic Circle at 10:00 a.m. on August 4 and toasted the event with champagne. I have a certificate to prove my crossing. Then it was on to Inuvik, on the Beaufort Sea (Arctic Ocean). We had two ferry crossings: one at Fort McPherson and one at Arctic Red River. Our bus had to be loaded on the ferry to make these crossings. Inuvik is at the end of the Dempster Highway, almost 100 miles from Dawson City. Permafrost makes it necessary for all buildings to be set on piles. This southern-style town of more than 3000 people, in the middle of the Arctic, is a true anomaly. In 1980, it was the largest community north of the Arctic Circle, with a hospital, a Royal Canadian Mounted Police unit, two radio stations, a newspaper, and two airports with daily jet service to southern Canada. You must keep in mind that I am writing this in 2013, so there may be differences now. Yes, it does get really cold in Inuvik in winter, with 60 to 70 degrees below zero Fahrenheit and a record, then, of 76 degrees below. When it's that cold they leave their motors running while they shop. Residents have reported nylon tires that were bald by the time they reached the airport a few miles from town.

Inuvik may be about as far as you can go when you travel north, but the dinner I had at the Eskimo Inn was second to none in the south. Arctic char, roast beef from Alberta, shrimp, smoked oysters, wild rice, chocolate mousse . . . . It was the best! The wine? Well, naturally it was White Bear. We flew over to Tuktoyaktuk one day. Tuk is right on the Arctic Ocean and I felt it my duty to stick my toes into those most northerly waters. Yes, It certainly was cold! Years later I did the same thing in Antarctica. Our lunch there consisted of caribou stew and ice cream. Their cuisine, shall we say, could not compare to that of Inuvik.

Next day our guide suggested a picnic by a pingo. I had no idea what a pingo was, but agreed when it was explained as a geological oddity. These ice-cored hills are used by locals as refrigerators during the summer months. The greatest concentration of these pingos in the world is found here in Canada's high Arctic. Tuk is the centrer of the Inuvialuit people. Prior to 1940 these aboriginal people lived in family camps along the shores of the Beaufort Sea. Today the community is the centrer for Beaufort Sea oil and gas explorations. (You must remember that I wrote this in 1980. The situation may be different now, in 2013.) In the winter, an ice road connects Aklavik (former seat of government for the western Arctic) and Inuvik. Tuktoyaktuk requires a short flight from Inuvik.

The Journey Itself

Update re Beaufort Sea (Wikipedia): "The sea, characterized by severe climate, is frozen over most of the year. Historically, only a narrow passage 100 km (62 miles) opened in August to September near its shores, but recently due to climate change in the Arctic, the ice-free area in late summer has greatly enlarged. The seacoast was populated about 30,000 years ago, but the population density is very low now. The sea contains significant resources of petroleum and natural gas under its shelf, such as the Amauligak field. They were discovered in the period between 1950s and 1980s, and their exploration became the major human activity in the area since the 1980s. The traditional occupations of fishery and whale and seal hunting are practiced only locally, and have no commercial significance. As a result, the sea hosts one of the largest colonies of beluga whales and there is no overfishing. There is a long-standing dispute between the United States and Canada over the sea border area, but significant steps were taken in 2010 toward this resolution."

Our last night in Inuvik included a grand evening at the Mad Trapper's Bar. It is famous for the decor. The walls were totally covered with Canadian dollar bills of every denomination. There may have been some US bills too, but I couldn't pick them out. Too much to drink? I don't think so. Just a couple of beers and a great time with our tour group at the end of a wonderful trip! I should add that there is a second reason for the bar's name. The Mad Trapper of Rat River was a man named Albert Johnson. In 1931, Johnson had been accused of sabotaging local traps, so an RCMP manhunt was out to get him. Parts of the legend attributed to the Mad Trapper were that he wore his snowshoes backwards, survived a dynamite explosion in his cabin, spent nights in a minus 40 degree wilderness, with no fire, and hunted for food...all of this while evading the police. He was finally shot from a plane by a WW1 fighter pilot ace. [Wikipedia]

Himalayan Kingdom of Tibet

Prior to 1982, and my first journey to India and Nepal, I was not aware of Tibet--the remote Himalayan kingdom, sometimes referred to as the Land of the Snows or the Land on the Roof of the World. In Nepal I had visited a Tibetan refugee camp, still unaware of the country itself or of its troubled past. It wasn't until my intended trip by rail across Siberia to China, with a side trip into Mongolia, was canceled that my travel agent suggested Tibet. So Tibet it was, and I set out on what turned out to be a marvelous adventure. I did not realize that foreign tourists were not allowed to enter Tibet until the death of Mao Tse-Tung and the overthrow of The Gang of Four, so this trip would be a real privilege for me.

Preplanning for a trip always involves acquiring someone to share accommodation, or a single supplement would add to the cost of the trip. My travel agent usually had a list of names of people who were doing the same trip. We picked a young girl from California who seemed like a good fit for me. Cathy was much younger than I, but socially active--even setting up meetings for political leaders in California. I verified that she would share with me. I would not meet her until we both arrived in Hong Kong, but that was okay with me. Former trips had gone well when I used the share option.

The Journey Itself

Another consideration is making certain that a traveller has the correct medical information and necessary pills for the country she will be visiting. Since Lhasa, Tibet's capital city, is 11,450 feet --one of the highest cities in the world--I was advised that I might require some pills to prevent "soroche," also known as altitude sickness. I had been at an altitude of this height when I visited Cuzco, in Peru, some years before, and despite the fact that Cuzco, is 11,000 feet above sea level, had no problem--no problem at all. Evidence of this was that my share partner and I were at the Black and White Disco the second night we were in Cuzco. The travel clinic at Toronto General Hospital suggested that Tibet might be different, so I did obtain medication to take with me, just in case.

All seemed to be in order, so my husband drove me to Pearson Airport, in Toronto. He always bid me goodbye with the same words, "Have a good trip and don't fall!" I confess to having a really bad record of falling, so his farewell words were warranted. We had done some travelling together, but most of the strange and exotic destinations I chose were definitely not for him. Nor were they any places my children would ever go. My son, who is an airline pilot, flew a plane home from Papua New Guinea and said, "I wouldn't even land in India, let alone choose it as a travel destination!" I call their choices "ho-hum" destinations.

My first flight was to Hong Kong, where our tour members would meet and spend the night. I settled into my room at a posh hotel and waited until California Cathy showed up. Many hours went by and I began to hope that I might become a "forced single"--single accommodation with no single supplement. That was too good to hope for, as Cathy showed up about 11:00 p.m. She seemed very nice, though a bit eccentric. She had met a guy on the plane and was going for drinks with him. However, she absolutely had to iron the skirt she wanted to wear.

The next day our group was headed for Guangzhou, a Chinese city located along the south coast of China with fast accessibility from Hong Kong. We were beginning to get to know our fellow travelers and discovered that we had a physician, a retired banker, another teacher, and a few others I can't remember. There was California Cathy, of course, carrying her pillow. She always did this, and I never knew why. Oh yes, I forgot to tell you that as we were preparing to leave the hotel, I noticed that Cathy had left her gold pendant on the counter in the bathroom. I called out to her, "Cathy you have forgotten your pendant, but don't worry--I am bringing it for you."

Her frantic reply was, "Oh no! You have touched it and it was blessed. Now the blessing is undone!" Right then I had a bad feeling that our partnership would not be a good one. As well, she had told me that she had just adopted Buddhism and had to chant for one hour each morning and night. Now, I have nothing against Buddhism. In fact I admire many of the tenets of that religion--witness the fact that I so admire the Dalai Lama. However, her chanting might prove to be a problem.

So it was on to Hangzhou for one day and overnight before we would fly to Chengdu. It was here in Hangzhou that Marilyn, a gal who had become my confidante, suggested that, although she was paying for a single, she would gladly share with me. She offered that I could tell Cathy that she (Marilyn) found that she did not like to be alone. I would share with her and Cathy could go as a single--with no extra charge. Deal accomplished, and I was very pleased.

On the flight to Chengdu I was seated with Dr. Ping and we discussed the need for taking the pills I had brought. He didn't think I'd need them, particularly given my Cuzco experience. He said he didn't like tour members to know he was a doctor or they would be constantly bothering him if they had any problems with their health. I agreed. We'd keep quiet on that point.

When we landed at the Gonggar Airport, in Tibet, it would be a one-hour ride by bus to Lhasa. Naturally we were all excited, but trying to adopt the advice given to all travelers to Tibet: "Take it slow and easy for the first day and give your body time to acclimatize." I was careful, but I noticed some of our group hurrying about to get photos of Tibetans we met at a rest stop on the road to Lhasa. Some would likely pay for it--and that is exactly what did happen. That night at dinner the older man in our group turned blue and fell off his chair. Everyone was concerned, but the doctor was taking care of things so Marilyn and I took off. Later that evening Dr. Ping said, "Heh, where did you guys go?" We just told him that we couldn't handle medical emergencies-- and indeed for me that was really true. As a child I used to faint in hospitals!

Our tour began the following day. Our tour group was accompanied by Annie, a national guide from Beijing. It was mandatory that she accompany us at every stage of our trip whether it be in China or Tibet. Our accommodation in Lhasa was at a Tibetan guest house. It was located in a military compound and we were forbidden to leave it at night or any other time without a Chinese guide. Obviously Chinese authorities wished to prevent any interaction between Western foreigners and local Tibetans.

Another indication of this distrust was the sign at the entrance to our Guest House. It read, "No Visitors." Our local guide, Tse dor-je, was permitted to take us to monasteries and temples, the Dalai Lama's winter palace (the Potala Palace), and his summer palace (the Norbulingka). As well, he took us on sightseeing trips out into the countryside, which included a yak ranch and a hydro station.

During my 1985 visit, I was unaware that most of the temples, shrines--even the Potala Palace, had been partially or totally destroyed. In fact, it has been recorded that more than 6000 of the country's monasteries and temples were ransacked and reduced to rubble. It seems that two senior Chinese party officials had visited Tibet in 1979 and were horrified at what they uncovered. Peking (Beijing) was forced to admit that the Chinese had made "a mess of things" in Tibet.

No one told us, but I did learn that restitution had already been made to the most sacred of all buildings: the Jokhang, the Sera and Drepung monasteries, and to the Potala and Norbulingka Palaces. Our guides were proud to point out their Public Works programs: roads, bridges, and power stations. Obviously we were shown only the sights that the Chinese wanted us to see--ones that would present them in a good light.

More than a million Tibetans died as a result of Chinese occupation. Thousands of Tibetans were arrested and many others deported, often to China. Large numbers of Chinese settlers were moved into Tibet. There were executions, beatings, public denunciations, and suicides. Identity cards were introduced for all, and freedom of movement severely curtailed. Monks were forced to abandon their calling, to marry and settle on the land, or starve. Temples and shrines were stripped of their sacred images and Buddhist scriptures burned. The great monastic universities in Lhasa were reduced to rubbish. Political indoctrination, at compulsory daily meetings, became part of the Tibetans' new way of life. All means of coercion were used to force them to abandon their old faith and embrace that of Marx and Mao.

At this point I have decided to spare you more of the terrible things that were inflicted on the Tibetans who remained in the homeland when the Dalai Lama fled for his life in 1959. Let me

The Journey Itself

just say they were unimaginable and horrific. I often wonder if what I experienced during my tour would have been different had I known what I do now.

Allow me to set all of that aside and proceed now with only some details of my 1985 trip, my interest in the country of Tibet and the culture of their beautiful people. Following is the account of my stay during my visit to the Land on the Roof of the World. The first visit was to the ancient Sera Monastery. It was here that we were able to observe the devotion of humble Tibetans, some of whom had possibly walked for days to arrive in Lhasa, the capital city of Tibet. Tibetans have been called the most religious people in the world. I must also inform you that their religion is not a matter of occasional ritual observances and acceptance of a particular code of belief and behavior. Religion to Tibetans has, for all of their recorded history, been an organic part of their everyday life.

Many pilgrims would begin the practice of prostrating themselves on the ground, standing again, moving ahead about a body length, and repeating this time and again as they circumambulated the city, or just the sacred building before they entered. I am not certain why this is done, but believe it is a form of reverence. I was told that men and women, even small children, mimicking their elders, practice this. As well, some very devout pilgrims are known to do this type of prostration, known as chang-cael, for miles as they approach the city.

We observed women walking down the streets of Lhasa twirling small prayer wheels. We were told that they are confident that, with every turn of the wheel, they will accumulate merit in this life and a better reincarnation in the next. I purchased a small prayer wheel and placed a thin paper inside, which reads, "Om Mani Padme Hum." This translates as, "Aum to the jewel in the lotus, hum." It is the mantra which is practiced most of all in the world and is heard everywhere in Tibet. I hope it is not sacrilegious for me to use it, as it is really just a keepsake. In the city, and when we were in Dharamsala later on, we saw rows of huge prayer wheels which Tibetans gave a twirl as they passed by. Women were carrying offerings of yak butter for the votive lamps that burn continuously in the monasteries and temples. A number of women ran after us shouting, "Dalai Lama! Dalai Lama!" I wondered what that was about, but our guide said they would be hoping we could give them a photo of His Holiness. Luckily we neither knew what they wanted or would have his picture, as giving out an image of the Dalai Lama could have made trouble for both of us.

As we entered the Sera Monastery it was very, very quiet, and the smell of the yak butter burning in the lamps induced a rather eerie, though respectful, feeling. We were led along to some rooms where Tibetan monks were turning the pages of books with wooden covers. At one point we passed a curtained holy place and were asked if we might like to look inside. I did, but cannot tell you that I saw anything; I only felt as though I might be looking into the Christian Ark of the Covenant. It was a very strange experience. Outside, on the balconies, we saw Tibetan families with beautiful children. Undoubtedly, theirs was a once in a lifetime pilgrimage to see the sacred buildings of Tibet.

The fourteenth Dalai Lama was selected as the reincarnation of the thirteenth Dalai Lama when he was only two years old. The regent, Reting Rinpoche, had a vision suggesting that Amdo would be the region where the next Dalai Lama would be found. The house they were looking for would have specific attributes: a one-story house with distinctive gutters and tiles. The search party carried various items with them. Some had actually belonged to the former Dalai Lama and some did not. These were given to the child to observe his reaction. In particular, one was alleged to be a walking stick; some were toys, and others were

The Journey Itself

certain relics that the former Dalai Lama owned. In each case the small child identified the real items saying, "That's mine! That's mine!" {Wikipedia}

On our third day in Lhasa we were taken to the famous Potala Palace, the winter palace of Tenzing Gyatso, the fourteenth Dalai Lama of Tibet. He would have lived there from a very early age though his formal confirmation took place when he was fifteen. The ancient palace, at 12,000 feet above sea level, was built by the fifth Dalai Lama in 1645, on the site of a smaller fortress that had been constructed in the seventh century.

We were required to climb another 1000 feet to view it. Some of the group, especially the smokers, were thankful that we had been given oxygen bags provided for the occasional quick puff as we climbed. The Potala is actually two palaces. The Red Palace is the center of religious worship; it houses the temples, shrines, and chorten (stupa). All of the Dalai Lamas since the Great Fifth have been buried at the Potala Palace. The White Palace is the living quarters of the monks, and acts as the administrative center of the Potala. It was the Red Palace that we were allowed to see. I have a photo of myself at the very top of the White Palace. I am standing beside an immense golden Dharma wheel and two sacred golden deer, one on either side of the wheel. The forbidden photo which I took of a small alcove, with yak butter lamps and other paraphernalia, will come up in the story of "Seeking the Dalai Lama."

Following visits to numerous other points of interest--the Drepung Monastery, Jokhang Temple (the most sacred in Tibet), the Barkor Square and Marketplace, and the Dalai Lama's Summer Palace (the Norbulingka)--I began to formulate some sense of the importance of the position of His Holiness the Fourteenth Dalai Lama. He is held in high esteem by the six million Tibetans for whom he acts as spiritual and temporal leader, despite the fact that he has been living in exile in Dharamsala, in northern India, since 1959.

During our stay in Lhasa, we were privileged to receive an invitation from our local guide. His very good friend was going to be married and we were invited to the reception, following the wedding. Since khatas are an expected gift for the bride and groom, my share partner Marilyn and I headed for a shop where these would be sold. The gift's price should reflect a person's status monetarily, so I selected a moderately priced white silk khata. When we arrived, we were presented to the bride and groom.

By this time they must have received a large number of guests, as they were both wearing a multitude of scarves. I took a number of pictures, which I promised to send to the parents of the happy couple and, a short time after I was home, Tse dor-je sent me a letter expressing the appreciation of all of the wedding party. The second part of the reception was a dance held in a large meeting room. They had recorded music, which included American tunes, and they all seemed very pleased that they could provide these for the foreigners. I must comment on the drinks they served. I believe it was called chang--or, as we called it, Tibetan beer. It was very strong and if you finished your glass, some serving girls ran quickly to give you a refill. It was obvious that I was obliged to sip slowly!

At the beginning of my story I mentioned our accommodation, but did not give you a description. It was a guest house, but a day or so after we were staying there we rated it as a "No Star Guest House." The bedding was so dirty that we slept in our clothes. Our room was up three flights of stairs and we had to pause frequently to get our breath. The decor? Spartan. Since my partner was a smoker, she used the oxygen pillow frequently, so I always told her that either she and the pillow would have to go out onto the balcony or she would not smoke. Marilyn was a really good sport, so it was no problem.

The difficulty at the guest house was that there was a third occupant. You guessed it. It was California Cathy! She had her own room but, as you will recall, she was required to chant morning and night. I won't give you any more details. Let's just say, "It was all about her!"

When we complained that we could hear her through the transom above the door that separated our rooms and were unable to sleep, she declared rather righteously, "Well, I have needs too!"

I hesitate to bore you with some words from the poem I wrote about "Leaving Lhasa," but will just add a few lines to indicate what an effect this trip had on me. We left at dawn so I will first set the scene, then express my feelings.

> A faint pink glow hints at dawn as we watch and reflect.
> Dark Himalayan peaks silhouette themselves
> Against a lightening sky.
> What do we hope to see--to remember?
> The holiest place on earth, set upon the roof of the world
> Has been our home for five brief days.
>
> Did the eerie experiences of visits to monasteries,
> The heavy scent of yak butter burning in votive lamps
> Heighten our senses?
> Did the many stacks of dusty sutras,
> The flag-like thangkas of Buddhas painted on silk
> Reveal to us another vision of our God?
>
> Suddenly the sun bursts through
> To illuminate the mountains, water and sky.

Himalayan Kingdom of Tibet

An exhilaration possesses us;
Thoughts of evil, enmity, worry, greed . . .
Disperse as nature unites with humanity
In a radiant rosy glow.
We leave Lhasa, spiritually enriched.
Visions of palaces, monasteries,
And beautiful Tibetan people
Indelibly etched in our minds
And held in our hearts
Forever!

        Barbara Street Brechin © 1985

Millionaire Homestays in Bombay

If you knew me, you would be amazed that I am writing a story with such a title. Surely, you will be thinking, a retired school teacher on the brink of entering her sixth decade would have no knowledge, let alone the skill or stamina, to become involved in such lunacy! Now that I reflect on my decision to do so, I too am dumbfounded. You, the reader, are not the first to pose the question, "What the heck were you thinking?"

When my good friend Krys proposed the possibility of my joining her on just such an adventure, I scoffed at the idea. Loved Kashmir; loved the Himalayas; but to actually do a trek? No way; couldn't imagine myself being able to do that. When she asked about my favorite destination of all my travels, to this point, I had always answered, "Kashmir. Unequivocally Kashmir!" And yes, I did have my own Arabian mare and was considered a moderately good rider--but a lengthy trek in the mountains was absolutely out of the question.

Krystyna's reply was, "You can do it, Barb. I'm certain of that." Krys hoped that she was beginning to wear me down, but apparently decided to let things gel for a while. I didn't know that she had already spoken to a Kashmiri guide named Bashir--even asked him to employ some cooks, guides, and pony men. She'd get everything in place, then spring it on me. In the end, I spoke to my long-suffering husband and children. The consensus was that it was a foolish idea. I had no camping experience, even here in Ontario. I couldn't walk long distances . . . and on and on.

Two weeks went by before the antagonist in this little drama called with another bit of information. Actually it was another carrot--an enticement I'd likely be unable to refuse. Krys had spoken with the former mayor of Bombay. Even more, coincidentally Mr. Joshi and two of his millionaire buddies would be pleased to entertain us in Mumbai, the current name for Bombay. The intention of this project was to set up homestays for Indian professionals in Canada, and for those Canadians with similar professions in India. Krys insisted that the opportunity for both of us was a once in a lifetime event. She did not see how I could possibly refuse. First the decadent life in Bombay, and then the exciting adventure in my favorite place in the whole world! What to do? What to do? Well, I guess you will realize by now that Madam Barbara, as the Indian people always called me, did finally give in to temptation. Miss Krystyna had finally won the day. The millionaires and the pony trek were on.

I'm always amazed to discover that the frustrations of flight delays, missed communications, and annoying transfers fade from one's memory soon after the trip is over. Not that the reader will care that much, but my diary recalls the litany of flight problems that Krys and I experienced while trying to get from Canada to Bombay. Makes me tired just reading the diary account…a two-hour delay aboard Air India flight 112 in New York; our panic with a sudden announcement at Heathrow, "Flight 112 boarding immediately." We had thought we had half an hour before we needed to be in the boarding lounge, so it was a real rush for us. Then there was a really long delay in New Delhi.

It should not have been a surprise, then, when no representative of the millionaires showed up to meet us. Apparently Mr.

The Journey Itself

Joshi's personnel manager had been at the airport at 2:00 a.m. and stayed until 5:00 a.m. We, of course, had been delayed so many times; it was not to his discredit that he had left. We tried to hail a cab which, in India, is not that easy to do. However, we finally managed to do so and arrived at the Kohinoor Airport Hotel in Bombay. It was thirty-six hours after our departure from Canada, and we were exhausted. Jet lag? Definitely, and a whole lot more. They say you should not lie down or sleep when jet-lagged, but we did take a half hour to adjust.

However, from that point on, we were treated like royalty. Bouquets of red roses adorned our hotel room; extravagant dinners, attended by no fewer than six servants at a time, gratified our every whim. For example, I drink Scotch straight with no water, just ice so when Mr. Joshi heard that he summoned a waiter to announce, "Quickly, Madam Barbara prefers her Scotch straight up!" This was certainly the life I should have been born to, and I was enjoying every minute of it.

Day two began with an air-conditioned cab for a wonderful lunch of Indian food at Copper Kettle and a shopping spree to search for sarees and Indian ready-made skirts and tops. We even purchased fashionable bindis (the red dot for the forehead that Indian ladies wear). I never did know if it meant you were married or single--just that the young gals wore it to make a fashion statement, and we certainly hoped to do that! What with the fancy dinner that night and the mayor's reception the next day, the visiting Canadians had to be ready to make an impression. Back to our room and a fresh bouquet of flowers, with time to rest and prepare for the evening.

We were entertained by all three millionaires at a superb dinner: Mr. Joshi (former mayor of Bombay, and condo owner), Mr. Pethie (high-end jewelry shop, construction company, and condo owner), and Mr. Kanitka (hotel owner). Surprisingly, this dinner was held at one of Mr. Joshi's Chinese restaurants. Yes, Chinese--in Bombay! The food was wonderful and after dinner we were asked if we might enjoy a liqueur. Krys refused, but I was eager to enjoy my favorite cognac. A Remy Martin was ordered and delivered by one of Mr. Joshi's young servants.

I have forgotten to mention one small disappointment. Mr. Jehanigeer, who I believe was involved in the Bollywood film industry, had hoped to entertain us at his beach house on the Arabian Sea but had been called away to another event. However, we were advised that during our next visit to Bombay, we would be expected to stay at said beach house. Krys and I agreed. We'd forgive him--just this once!

On day three, Namrata, Mr. Joshi's lovely daughter, came with an air-conditioned limo to transport us to their residence at Ocean View Apartments. The entire tenth floor was what the Joshi family called home: very nice, quite modern, with servants everywhere, to open doors and wait upon our every need. Mrs. Joshi (Anagha) did not eat with the rest of the family and guests, as she was busy serving. Apparently she did all of the cooking too, as Manahor does not like other people's food. Since they don't use utensils as we do, I recall having some difficulty eating with my hands. However, the food was superb and I don't believe I embarrassed myself in my attempt to fit in!

Day four was to be very special, as this was the day of the mayor's reception and breakfast at his bungalow on the Indian Ocean. We had been assigned to the bedroom of the Joshis' younger daughter, Namrata. It was quite pleasant to awaken with a warm ocean breeze wafting into our room and someone playing exquisite music on an Indian sitar. Turned out to be Unmesh, the daughter whose wedding would be several months after our visit. Side bar: We were invited to the wedding, but obviously would not be able to attend. The Joshi parents were proud to display all of the wedding sarees and gifts of gold jewelry...a really big thing for an Indian bride-to-be.

Following a traditional Maharashtra breakfast consisting of a delightful tea and biscuits, we said our goodbyes, then on to the mayor's bungalow, by air-conditioned limo, of course. What did I wear? In one of the photos taken that day, I am pictured in my long red and green cotton skirt with matching overblouse and long cotton scarf over one shoulder. Did I wear the bindi? Of course. The picture shows the mayor on my right and his wife on the left. Guess I really didn't look Indian, but I had tried. We were received and taken out to be seated on the lawn in beautiful wicker chairs, overlooking the Arabian Sea. The press arrived to take photos of the distinguished Canadian guests, and Krys and I enjoyed a casual conversation with our host. Next, we were presented with City of Bombay gold medals, a book about Bombay, and gorgeous bouquets of red roses. Servants came then to take us for breakfast with the mayor and his wife. Another breakfast? Yes, and it wouldn't be the last, as this was the day of three breakfasts!

Then, Mr. Joshi's driver delivered us to the home of Mr. Pethie, our second millionaire host. His humble abode--and I use the term with a certain amount of irony--was a double penthouse apartment! Krys and I were definitely impressed. Mrs. Pethie graciously offered us breakfast. Yes, a second breakfast, which we respectfully refused. We did, however, accept an invitation to attend a pooja--a ceremony that is part of Indian wedding rituals.

Mr. Pethie's brother and family were celebrating the marriage of his son to a very beautiful young Indian woman. They were anxious for the Canadian ladies to witness this joyous occasion, so we just went down to the fifth floor of this same magnificent apartment complex. After the religious segment of the affair, we were treated to a viewing of a lovely video, which displayed the bride's dress and amazing display of gold jewelry. Once again there was the offer to partake of some of the Indian delicacies which had been prepared for the pooja. It would have been rude to refuse, so we did sample a few of the goodies. By this time it was past noon, so probably it didn't count as breakfast.

A visit to one of Mr. Pethie's older jewelry shops in Dadar was next on the list. His teenage son, Sameer, took us there for a short viewing of the wonderful collection of jewelery. I was afraid to ask the cost, and was dilly-dallying about the selection of any particular item, when the manager suggested that he had been advised that Mr. Pethie would bring a few things home. That way we could relax and make decisions at our leisure. It was Mr. Pethie's turn to host a late dinner that night. Again it was at a Chinese restaurant. What is it with these Indian men and Chinese food? My diary isn't too specific, but there is definitely mention of tasty hors d'oeuvres, lobster, prawns, shrimp, and Chinese dishes to die for! Beverage? Can't recall if we had wine, but rather doubt it. Perhaps I was tricked into a Scotch, though!

The morning of the following day was spent relaxing with Mr. and Mrs. Pethie and son Sameer. A display of jewelry was laid out on the dining room table and Krys and I were free to choose, or not, any of the items that might appeal to us. I can't speak for Krys, but I did pick a silver bracelet with an interesting Indian motif. During our conversation about Kashmir, Sameer said he'd really like to go with us, but wasn't free to do so.

Mr. Kanitka, youngest of the three millionaires--or Kani, as he had asked us to call him--sent a hotel van to Pethie's to transport us to his home in a suburb of Bombay. He and his wife lived in a condo-type building where residents were all of the same caste. You may be wondering if the caste system still exists

The Journey Itself

in India. That was 1989, but I doubt that things have changed much even now. Aparna, Kani's wife, treated us to a refreshing cold drink and explained that she had arranged a program for us at a private school. Since Krys and I were both teachers, she had assumed that we would be interested, and it would be a great opportunity for the students to perform for us. We were received with great flair and warmth. The smallest children (aged three to six) sang and danced and we were presented with water and roses. No, we did not dare to drink the water! We just made a respectful pretense of doing so.

The teachers were proud of their school, pointing out all of the many wonders that they could perform. God knows how, with practically no books, a few tiny blackboards, and one larger blackboard for the teacher. By the time we got to the second school, we had grown desperately tired. The heat, lack of fluids, and pace were taking their toll. Complaining, were we? That's true, but you are likely saying, "No one ever said being a celebrity would be easy!" To you I must reply, "Touché. Touché."

Omar Sada Kanitka, or Kani as you know him by now, drove us into the city for some time on our own. His recommendations were that we might enjoy some time at the Centaur Hotel--perhaps a swim at their pool, or shopping nearby. This set us up for a couple of unfortunate taxi experiences. The first took us to the wrong Centaur Hotel--the Beach Centaur Hotel, not the Airport Centaur Hotel--and the cab we chose next refused to turn the meter on...a definite no-no when travelling anywhere in the world. We jumped out of that cab, hailed another, and finally made it to the right Centaur.

The balance of our last day in Bombay was orchestrated by Kani. Not to diminish our respect for the other two millionaires, but Krys and I definitely enjoyed Mr. Kanitka's company the most. He was, may I say, not just younger and more cosmopolitan, but handsome to boot. The fact that he ran the whole show at his Kohinor Hotel didn't hurt either. Roses in our suite, room service whenever we wished, laundry, a great lunch, all flight arrangements and, as a grand finale, a splendid dinner with the boss! Not Chinese, but every Indian dish we'd ever heard of, and some we hadn't. Wine had been discussed the night we spent at his home, and our favorites had been ordered specifically for our pleasure.

While staying in Kashmir, Moghul Emperor Jehangeer once declared, "If there be Paradise on earth, it is here, it is here!" So, with our millionaire's homestay over, Madam Barbara and Miss Krystyna were set to fly to Paradise at six a.m. the next morning.

Pony Trek in the Himalayas

For those of you who may be wondering why I have always been so fascinated by Kashmir, I admit to having no definitive answer. During my first visit to this remarkable destination and again on this one, the identical emotions arose. Why was it that I seemed unable to restrain myself from shedding a few tears? I'd been in many beautiful places before. What is it that this alleged paradise provides that others do not?

As a small child, my mother had always told me stories about her brother, Lt. Col. R.C. Phelps. I knew that he had served with the Royal Medical Corps, first on a hospital ship in the Mediterranean during World War I, then in India and Burma, with the Indian Medical Service. In 1929, he transferred to the Civil Medical Service in Burma, where he was in charge of a hospital located on the Burma Road, thirty miles back in the hills from Mandalay. When Britain declared war on Japan, he was placed in charge of the Burma Military Hospital in Maymyo, as well as his own establishment. Finally, with the fall of Singapore, the Japs (as Uncle Roy always named them), closed in on Maymyo from both sides on the Burma Road. The sick and wounded were evacuated by air; the rest, my uncle among them, set out on the long hike to India. Though thousands died along the way, my uncle did make it to India and was on one of the last planes to fly out to safety.

Pony Trek in the Himalayas

Every five years Uncle Roy was able to spend a year's leave back in Merritton--at the Phelps ancestral home. This is where I was introduced to all things Burmese and Indian. With no television, magazines, or books to afford such an in-depth portrayal of these interesting countries, I had it all--first hand. His stories were fascinating, his photographs marvelous! Many of the Taj Mahal, the Himalayas, and Kashmir were displayed prominently on the walls of my grandparents' home. As an adult, I accused him of having a love affair with these places. Could it be possible that I too had subconsciously developed an inexplicable affection for India and Kashmir?

Some people love the oceans; with me it is definitely the mountains. Just to be in that environment stirs the same feelings of wonder--a certain euphoria and if it's the Himalayas--tears. So, now that you may be convinced that I am mildly deranged, perhaps you would like me to continue the story. To this point, I have been remiss in neglecting to divulge the real purpose of the Kashmir segment of this trip. Krys and I had previously organized some group trips for my newly incorporated Connoisseur Travelplan Enterprises, Inc. In fact, the first tour of China, Hong Kong, and Thailand, in 1988, had been quite successful--so much so that the organization of Indian Millionaire Homestays, in Canada, had come next and the more venturesome pony-trekking groups would follow. Obviously, trekking in the Himalayas would appeal to a younger, more physically active clientele. So why was I going to check this out? Didn't I tell you that I was almost sixty? Oops! I did say that, didn't I? Well, "No fool like an old...." You know the rest!

What neither of us knew, possibly even the houseboat owners, shopkeepers, rug and furniture craftsmen--even the organizers of treks--was that within three years, their mountain paradise of Kashmir was about to metamorphose into a country battered by army repression, police violence, and merciless terrorism. The

THE JOURNEY ITSELF

sound of gunshots, over the hitherto placid waters of Dal Lake, would replace the Muslim calls to prayer and the gentle dip of Shikara paddles in the quiet water.

Tourism, Kashmir's biggest source of income, would drop from 1500 to 15 people per day. Houseboats would lie vacant. There would be no need for shikaras to paddle tourists across the lake or along the gentle river that leads to the early-morning market for vegetables, fruits, and flowers. All of the cheerful salesmen at the Aziz Kashmiri Rug Factory would be idly sitting at their homes. The young men and women who worked long hours crafting rugs like the one that hangs in my Indian dining room--pure silk with 700 knots per square inch--what would they be doing? And Uncle Abdul, who sold me those other two wonderful rugs that enhance my bed-sitting room...he'd be out of business! The papier-mâché vendors, the sellers of tablecloths, peddlers of Limka (a popular soft drink), even a young man with furs--they would not be arriving at the Arizona houseboat. I can hear them now as they would step up onto our verandah saying, "No need to buy! Only look!"

In perusing my souvenirs of the last visit to Kashmir, I came across a letter from the trekking guide. It is dated 1991--only two years after we had been there. A heavy-hearted young man was describing their business situation in this manner: "Since one and a half years, we had no business. All the time curfew. The violence is between the Indian army and civilians." Despite this, his optimism for some groups still going to Kashmir was repeated throughout his letter. He maintained that they were hearing that the Indian government was progressing with restoration of business for Kashmiris. Finally, toward the end of his communication, came the real reason for his letter. "Lot of troubles, lot of failing going on here and there. Would you mind help me? I would like to borrow some money from you. When you come back, I will hand over to you and I am sure I will have business this year."

I hope the reader will not think less of me when I say that I did not send Bashir any money. I realized, even then, that no amount of money could possibly save my Kashmiri friends from the destitution that was to be their fate. Newspaper articles, here in Canada, were recounting that houseboat owners were having to sell their beautiful rugs and other furnishings just to survive. Poor Bashir. Poor Yousuf--owner of Arizona. Poor Ajaz Wafai--the tablecloth man who took us by shikara to visit his two grandmothers! What must have happened to them?

The flight from New Delhi to Srinigar was uneventful, except for the fact that Krys and I had enjoyed an interesting conversation with a young businessman named Tariq. His home was near Srinigar and he would be happy to have us attend his wedding. What is it with these Indian people? Is it possible that Krys and I have a sign on our foreheads that reads, "Please invite us to your wedding"? Anyway, it wouldn't take place until we had returned from the trek, so it might be a possibility--and a chance to wear our new saris!

We were met at the airport by one of the servants from Houseboat Arizona. A short shikara ride brought us to the houseboat, where we were greeted by Krystyna's friend Bashir. He was a handsome young man who exuded charm and confidence. I was momentarily able to curtail my growing concern about the trek. We had five days to experience the luxury of houseboat living in Kashmir.

The deluxe houseboats: Holiday Inn, Meena Bazaar, Taj Mahal, Golden Palace . . . are all accessible by shikaras (gondolas) with equally exotic names: Heaven of Flowers, Morning Star, Golden Eagle--even a motor boat named Boeing 747. We never did use the motor boat...way too fast for us! These houseboats, which are permanently moored in a long ragged line along the fringes of the beautiful Dal and Nagin Lakes, are too large to permit ease of movement. Hence, the development of Kashmir's version of extravagant living in the marvelous setting exalted by the rich and famous--even kings!

Though not quite as luxurious as Meena Bazaar, where I had stayed in 1982, Arizona was quite lovely. Picture, if you will, a verandah that overhangs the large square-ended hull and leads into the beautifully appointed living room. It is furnished with attractively crafted walnut wood furniture, delicately woven Indian carpets, and numerous items of Indian silver. Beyond the living room is a fine dining room--again with marvelous walnut table, chairs and buffet. Above the table, a sparkling chandelier! Still further along the corridor are two large bedrooms and a great bathroom, complete with huge tub and shower. At a discreet distance is the cook boat, source of all our meals. The families' quarters are also beyond the main houseboat.

That night, after dinner, Bashir suggested a shikara ride on the Dal Lake. Leaning back against the shikara cushions and positioned between Krys and myself, I believe Bashir may have been, if not in Paradise, then a very happy Maharajah! A moonlit night, with only the sound of the shikara paddle dipping into the peaceful water, the twinkling lights at Nehru Park . . . . Who could resist? Certainly not I. Kashmir had worked its magic--again! Any apprehension about trekking in the Himalayas mystically disappeared. And, if that wasn't enough, a gin and tonic, plus a little wine, finished off with just a smidgin of cognac, certainly put us all in a good mood!

Only three more days remained until departure day - just a brief time for Krys and I to laze about and defer to final preparations for the pony trek. Actually, not much was required of us, as Bashir had done all of this before we arrived. Our days began with a delightful breakfast, served in the dining room, followed by time up on the roof, listening to tapes, writing postcards, and enjoying all of the shikara traffic that passed by Arizona. If it was too hot, Yousuf would put up the awning. He was such a thoughtful guy.

Yousuf invited us to accompany him and some of the servants on a shikara trip to visit the early- morning market. I have a wonderful video of this trip. Had you been with us, you would have reveled in the scenery. Our shikara passed along the quiet river, through poplar avenues, and past Kashmiri homes and shops to the point in the river where all of the vendors had congregated. Our shikara would be moved next to the one that was selling what Yousuf wished to purchase. The proverbial bargaining ensued; then it was on to the next. Yousuf selected wonderful fruits and vegetables--even gorgeous lotus flowers for our dining table.

Our formal dinner was often served up top. A dining table rested on a beautiful Indian carpet; candles, on the table and in standards nearby, flickered in the darkness. Gulam, the servant who had been on Meena Bazaar during my former houseboat stay, was main server for the evening. I believe Yousuf had told him I was back and had invited him for that special evening. Imagine my surprise as he came up the stairs! On my last trip he had been so attentive—he even brought special tea and other treatments to my room one night when I was ill. Treatments? Okay, I turned down the massage with alleged magical properties!

Yousuf was chuckling with delight. "You know this gentleman, Madam Barbara?" I told him that I certainly did, and that I thanked him so much for planning that detail. The following day, all last-minute preparations had to be made. We were sitting in the

The Journey Itself

living room as Bashir checked our gear. As he identified each item, the reality of what I had agreed to do began to set in. I was definitely having second thoughts. What was I thinking? Could I do this thing? What if I just stayed back and let Krys go alone? I decided to voice my concern. Both Krys and Bashir assured me that I'd be fine. I could probably ride the pony most of the time, and there would be lots of help from the whole entourage. Truth be told, I couldn't see myself letting Krys down, so I acquiesced. My Himalayan dream was about to come true--or not!

If the horrendous taxi ride from Dal Lake to Sonamarg was to be any indication of the hazards I might expect on the actual trek, I was already in trouble! The driver displayed definite signs of road rage. I wasn't able to interpret his Hindi outbursts, but I knew they weren't complimentary to the drivers of the other cars we passed--and we passed everything! Obviously, a sign that read, "Drive like hell, you're sure to get there!" was not going to impede this fearless guy.

About halfway into our journey he stopped the car, got out, and announced, "Flat tire." It would take an hour to get it fixed, so, rather than standing around, Bashir suggested that we walk for a while. We were about half an hour from our lunch stop, so we pressed on. The little shop at Kangan was, to say the least, a disappointment. Unless you think tea, a slice of bread, a cold potato, and a really hard boiled blue egg is delightful fare, you would have given a similar rating to our lunch.

We resumed our walk for another half hour until our cab pulled up to deliver us to Sonamarg. I didn't realize it at the time but, as I was beginning to write this, I discovered a magnificent photo that Uncle Roy had taken of a camp he'd stayed at back in the 1930s. Written on the back of the picture, in his handwriting, a single word: Sonamarg. Coincidence? I think not. Bashir had chosen this spot for our overnight campsite. It was here that we would meet our pony men with their ponies, the cooks, and the other guides who would make up the entire entourage.

Our candlelight dinner was served in the kitchen tent. The Kashmiri cooks, as is their custom, were sitting on their haunches, enjoying our pleasure. It was a truly beautiful night, with a full moon, and only the sound of the Lidden River rushing by. Sounds perfect for a peaceful night of undisturbed sleep, doesn't it? Wrong! Novice camper that I was, I had not had the forethought to bring other than a ground sheet to protect me from the rocks. So, although my sleeping bag was warm and cozy, I slept very little.

Day one of the trek found Madam Barbara with a sore throat and visions of it worsening. Another bad omen? Possibly, but I was determined to set this aside and hope for the best. Seated on my pony, as it picked its way along the trail, I was enthralled by the mountains--my mountains, the Himalayas! The poet C. Day Lewis, wrote that it is not easy to possess the Himalayas of the mind. Agreed. However, it would be the real Himalayas that I hoped to conquer. Not really conquer…just enjoy! If the first two hours were any indication of the pleasures that lay ahead, this adventure would be splendid. Dusky blue mountain peaks rose into an azure sky. In the distance, the dark green of evergreens and yellow-green of deciduous trees still filled the landscape. An occasional hawk or lammergeyer soared above us. Following is my diary entry for that morning. "As we rode higher and higher, the valley receded; the mountain paths narrowed; in the distance, the majestic peaks seemed to become our equals. My heart sang with the joy of that quintessential experience, high in the Himalayas! Yes, truly, this above all places on earth, must be the home of the gods!"

Little did I realize that the euphoria of that moment was soon destined to dissipate. Our first rest stop had been located beneath some huge trees, but now we were much higher and there were no trees. My video camera and expensive Pentax still camera were looped over the horn of my little Nadu's saddle and, at one narrow point on the mountain's edge, the pony tripped. Little Bashir always held my arm so I didn't fall off. However, my precious equipment narrowly missed a tragic plunge into eternity.

Krys and the rest of the entourage were some distance ahead. I could see her nonchalantly striding ahead as if she were out for a Sunday walk on the promenade. Nothing ever bothered her. She had great stamina, and could eat any food, even the spiciest Indian dishes. Little wonder that she and Bashir expected I'd be able to do the trek. You, the reader, may recall though that I was fifty-nine, I had never camped before and certainly never attempted a trek!

My pony man was also named Bashir. He had very little English. Make that, "Madam, problem" or "No problem?" I could tell that he was anxious, for those words were repeated over and over again. I wanted to shout, "There is a problem, and it's a big one. I should never have come on this damn trek!" Excuse the language.

As the afternoon wore on, our route opened into a more level terrain, but it was wall-to-wall rocks and I was no longer able to ride. Picture, if you will, Madam Barbara struggling to navigate over huge rocks, impeded by sore throat, headache, feeling the altitude, and all. An inner voice whispered, "So how do you like your Himalayas now?" I was definitely falling behind and Bashir and Krys were shouting, "Come on, Barb; you can do it. Soon we will stop for tea." I knew Bashir's definition for soon could not possibly match mine. The sea of rocks stretched from side to side. I was definitely between a rock…and…another rock. Krys admitted, later that night, that she was worried about me. She said my face was as white as an enamel basin.

Pony Trek in the Himalayas

We finally arrived at the camp site six hours after our beginning at Sonamarg. Krys had walked most of the way, but was still in remarkably good condition. I, on the other hand, was considering my options. Continue for six more days, rest a half day to see if I improved--then continue on, (Bashir's idea), get lifted out by helicopter, (Barb's idea--not really a choice), or go back to Sonamarg to get transportation to the houseboats at Dal Lake. My decision would have to be made that night, so I was unable to think of anything else. I have a photo that Krys took of me in our tent that night before dinner. Madam Barbara was definitely one sick puppy. Her bright red face was indicative of a high fever, but still smiling for the camera. The one I took of Krys showed her applying a coat of nail polish! No worries for her!

We got wind of two other trekkers whose tent had been soaked by a downpour the night before and my spirits rose just a bit. They might be going down to Sonamarg the next day, and I'd have company--not just the little pony man Bashir had selected, if I made that choice. Supper was again served in the kitchen tent. The Polish and German gentlemen joined us and provision was made for one of the guests to sleep in Bashir's tent; the other would sleep with the cooks, and Bashir was to sleep in our tent. We sat drinking tea and rum for several hours after supper and my condition didn't seem quite so desperate. However, there was only one possibility for me: I'd have to turn back!

In all of my travels to Asia, I've been in some flagrantly bad situations: pushed from side to side by revelers on the wall in Xian to the point where I almost went over, the evening in a spirit House in Papua New Guinea with locals who had been headhunters in the early 1900s, and the flight into Tibet on a seriously ancient Chinese airplane with altitude sickness a distinct possibility if/when we landed...desperately sick with dysentery in Dharamsala, India and Jaisalmer, Rajasthan and fearful that

I had contracted malaria in Thailand. There were others, but I'd never been so afraid!

After breakfast the next morning, Krys separated the stuff she would be carrying with her and Bashir introduced me to my new pony man. Rashid had little English, so Bashir provided him with a small note--written in Hindi. Allegedly the memo, which he tucked into the pocket of Rashid's old suit jacket, was my ticket to safety. I was so nervous that six trips behind the rocks (a trekker's bathroom) were required before Rashid could hoist me onto Nadu, his little horse of 15 years. People talk about their moment of truth. This was mine! Let's just say, travel insurance would not be an issue if Madam Barbara disappeared from the trek. When I got home my daughter said, "Your pony man could just have said, 'What lady? I don't remember a lady called Barbara!'"

From my diary: "I know that I have never been so frightened in all my life--never! The ocean of rocks that lies ahead--my God--how will we ever get through? I certainly can't walk--tried that yesterday and have the bruises to prove it. However, I must put my trust in Rashid, the gods of the Himalyas and my own God. Our little retinue included: Bulba (pack horse), Tota (the baby colt), Madam Barbara aboard Nadu, and Rashid steadying me as he walked alongside.

With yesterday's endurance test, about five hours in the saddle, my seat was really sore; my knees hurt from leaning forward on steep ascents and pushing back on the descents. I had a large blood blister on the little finger of my right hand--the result of desperately gripping the metal hand horn of the saddle. Rashid held the reins and my arm in really difficult places. I expected to have a huge bruise where he did that, but I was grateful for his help. His English was pretty much like Little Bashir's: "Madam? Problem?" or "No problem?"

Rashid must have been taking another route, as I was able to stay aboard Nadu as he crossed several shallow rivers and navigated through oceans of rocks. Paths circling the mountains gave a frightening view of valleys and river beds that lay thousands of feet below. I scarcely dared to look! I do recall saying to myself, "What kind of fool would get into this dangerous predicament?" Rashid kept saying, "Problem Madam?" or "No Problem?" I nearly always replied that there was no problem or that I was okay.

Some hours later he announced, "Rocks finish!" Even more English, I thought. Hurrah for Rashid! Gradually the stark grey of rocks and the cold blue of streams gave way to bits of green in the distance. Then it was lichens and mosses, which grow in the third climatic zone. Little by little alpine scrub, shrubs, and bushes bordered our trail and, an hour later, the beautiful forests welcomed our progress. For a half hour or so Rashid kept saying "Few minutes. Few minutes." And suddenly we were there: the very spot where we had rested on the way up. Stately pine and fir trees, wonderful bamboo and gorgeous rhododendrons! In fact, if you will recall, I had agreed with the Kashmiris who avow it to be the home of the gods.

Rashid indicated that we would have lunch here, so I dismounted. I wish I had taken a picture, but Krys now had my Pentax and video camera. Rashid was a small man dressed in the usual Kashmiri baggy pants, tied with a cord, soaked tunic-type top, and a very old yellow sweater. His dirty old suit jacket remained tied to one of the ponies. His shoes? As I recall, they were plastic sandals. So much for Western trekking gear!

Rashid now produced our lunches and we sat cross-legged beneath one of the fir trees. I removed my Tilley hat and set it on the ground next to me. Someone, it might have been me, had sat on my cardboard lunch box because I opened it to discover a squashed blue potato, a piece of bread, a very hard boiled blue egg, and a rather limp carrot! Anyway, as we enjoyed our meal, and I use the term loosely, Rashid picked up my hat and tried it on. I was effusive in my appreciation of how he looked, and he must have assumed that said hat was now his! I let it go, as I described in an article I wrote for Tilley's catalogue, "I would have given him 100 Tilley hats if he was successful in returning me to safety."

We weren't there yet, though we were within sight of the highway. We encountered a large group of students out for a day trek and then moved down to the road. Five of the kids were calling out, "Pen! Pen! Pen for school!" I'd heard this so many times before, particularly in Nepal. No sir, I thought, I need this pen to record what happened to the foolish madam who went all the way to her beloved Kashmir, only to have to turn back and miss the best of it. Rashid indicated that I should get back on Nadu and he would follow with the other ponies. I should tell you that this was a busy route for army trucks going up to Leh, where there was a great deal of unrest. I was in the midst of all of this traffic, on my pony, with honking horns and speeding traffic. It was 1989, so Kashmir was not so involved yet. So, Barb was on her pony. Rashid was wearing her Tilley hat and following with the ponies. He gave my Nadu a whack on the rump--and I was off! Cars and trucks were whizzing by, barely missing the crazy foreign lady. The really hot sun was beaming down on my head, so I motioned to Rashid that I needed my hat. He readily obliged my request, though he couldn't have known that I had every intention of leaving it with him.

About fifteen minutes later, we arrived at Sonamarg Hotel. I was shown to a table on the patio and Rashid began his search for my ride back to the houseboats at the Dal Lake. In case you have forgotten, I was very sick, with a temperature of at least 102 F; I had no money and was at the mercy of Rashid's ability

Pony Trek in the Himalayas

to get me a ride. A kind gentleman came out from the hotel to take my order and, despite my announcement that I couldn't pay, brought me a pot of tea. From my vantage point I was able to see Rashid showing the note (written in Hindi) to various people, all of whom were shaking their heads in the negative. One person, who spoke English, said something about a bus and four hours. I was not sure if it would take four hours to get to Srinigar, or if it wouldn't arrive for four hours. Since I had my tent and a whole bunch of gear, I hoped it wouldn't end up with me, on a bus. Finally a young fellow, with a straw hat jauntily cocked on one side of his head, was nodding his head in the affirmative, and I was summoned to come to his car. He and my pony man loaded me and my stuff into the taxi.

The tent was in a metal box in the trunk, and my junk was all around me in the back seat. Hairy now had the famous note-- my passport to safety. I gave Rashid the hat and we were off. My new friend, Hairy, was very talkative. You may be wondering how I had acquired his name so early into our relationship. I didn't find out his real name until later. Hairy just seemed so appropriate for a guy who, time and again, checked his hair in the rear view mirror. Okay, his long, wavy black hair did warrant repeated attention, and his mustache and short black beard were carefully kept. He put on American tapes, probably to please me or to show off a bit, and began asking some rather personal questions: "Are you married?" "Where is your husband?" and "How old are you?" My answers were relatively truthful-- except for the age!

As you read this, you are very likely questioning my vulnerability: a Canadian lady entrusting herself to a total stranger who was Muslim, young, and very good-looking. I must confess that the thought never entered my head. I was allegedly on my way to the safety of the houseboats on Dal Lake. However, I did take pause at Hairy's erratic driving and signs we passed that said,

"Drive like hell! You're sure to get there!" Remember, too, that I had no money to pay him. I wondered how I'd handle the situation when he found that out but put it out of my mind for the time being. I was one step closer to safety! Nothing else seemed to matter.

An hour later we picked up another passenger--a very pretty young female teacher who obviously knew Hairy and called him by his real name: Aktar. She was traveling to a village about half an hour away where she owned a small shop. They began speaking Hindi so, although I was able to interpret their body language, the conversation was unknowable to me. Apparently, Aktar was quite the flirt as he spoke to her, laughing and looking her up and down all the time. She laughed too, though she feigned a certain shyness for appearances' sake. Aktar apologized that they were speaking Hindi, but that was fine with me as I was totally exhausted and still feeling quite ill. However, when he decided to put on more American tapes, I happily agreed. They were all love songs, undoubtedly selected to impress the other gal, but I enjoyed them too. I don't recall the names--only one line: "You said you would love me forever." How many women have found this forever thing to be untrue? After all, as one of my young gentleman friends advised me, "Forever is a very long time!"

When Aktar dropped his other passenger off, we were alone again. He put on Indian music and fell silent for a while. The ride to Srinigar was becoming tiresome. My head ached and my fever persisted. Aktar had purchased a Limka cold drink for me at a little shop, as I was definitely dehydrated. I was barely able to appreciate the beautiful scenery. Mountains in the distance, brilliant green rice fields, gentle rivers, and small villages, with their tiny shops and interesting people, all became a blur. I seemed almost oblivious to my beloved Kashmir. However, it was difficult to ignore the traffic. Buses, cars, carts--all seemed to miss each other, though I could never figure out why. Horns were blown continuously to announce the desire to pass, and vehicles whipped around each other even though there could be a car, bus, or truck coming the other way. I could never understand what all of the hurry was about! Must be an Indian thing. I'd seen the same in New Delhi and Bombay.

I have forgotten to explain the reason for military presence in Leh, and Kashmir. It is necessitated by their geographical location on the uneasy borders of Pakistan, USSR, Afghanistan, and China. All of these countries would dearly love to acquire the above-mentioned lands. In 1988, terrorists set off numerous explosions in Srinigar and in Leh. The report of three or four deaths was seriously under-reported, as it was more like thirty or forty! I can sense the reader's disbelief that I would put myself in such a dangerous situation. Allow me to plead ignorance. My good friend, Miss Krystyna, had neglected to mention any of this! I'll give her the benefit of the doubt, though. Perhaps Bashir hadn't mentioned it to her.

Finally, Aktar brought me to Nehru Park, which was within sight of Houseboat Arizona--within sight, but across the lake. I'd need a shikara ride to get there. The magic note was shown again to all shikara owners but all declared reluctance, if not refusal, to carry us across. Even worse, some of the houseboat owner's friends announced that Yousuf had gone to the market. He was not at home! That didn't mean so much to Aktar, as he was demanding his 400 rupees for the taxi ride from Sonamarg. All he wanted was his pay, and he'd be on his way. At this point I had to confess that I had no money with me, and that all I'd need to do was get back to the houseboat, go in, and secure what was needed for the shikara man and Aktar.

I must have looked honest enough, as we all got into the shikara and headed for Arizona. I had no back-up plan, but I was

The Journey Itself

desperate. When we arrived at the houseboat, I climbed the steps up to the verandah and strode through the living room and dining room to our bedroom. The two payees remained in the shikara. I spent a short time allegedly getting my money, which had been left with Yousuf for safekeeping. Only he would know where it was. Finally Madam Barbara had to go out and face the music. To put it mildly, all hell broke loose! Shikara man and taxi man went nuts, shouting at the top of their lungs and threatening me with who knows what. I was not too sure what, as they had both lapsed into their mother tongues!

Fortunately, some of Yousuf's relatives came to see what was going on. After they had paid both men and sent them on their way, they were anxious to know how they might help. Perhaps I needed a doctor or to go to the hospital. Side bar: I'd seen Indian hospitals and definitely didn't want to see one of their doctors. I'd have to be really, really sick to agree to either of these options! All I wanted was to have a good hot bath and to crash spread-eagled on my bed.

Since a bath would require starting a fire to heat the water, I settled for a cup of tea before I did just that...collapsed on my bed. I recall my thoughts vividly. I am safe! Safe at the houseboat! A few days and I'll feel better. All I need is a rest for this poor old body!

A sadness came over me when I finally wrote about this the next day. Sadness and a few tears. We may not remain forever young. Try as we may, it is not possible. The house of the spirit grows old and weak. Only the mind is free to fly high above those mighty Himalayan peaks, or to climb the mountains, to rest in mountain pastures and beside mountain lakes and rivers. So sad ...so sad! There would be a week or more for me to recover aboard Arizona, and Yousuf made every attempt to take good care of me. Do I sense that the reader may be questioning my real safety? I was alone on a houseboat with any number of Muslim men about - Yousuf on Arizona, and numerous others on adjacent houseboats. Let me explain. Krys and I were proposing to bring groups from Canada. We'd both been in Kashmir before and were expected to tout the area as a great destination. Kashmiris could not afford any bad press!

I wakened several times in the night and knew that I certainly was ill. My nose was running, I was coughing, and worst of all, I had serious diarrhea. Despite all of this I was able to return to dreamland and slept until 9:30. I realized that I would need to present myself if I wanted breakfast, so I took a shower (cold, of course) and washed my hair. Most of all, I wanted water! I was so thirsty and desperately in need of fluids. I'd been this sick in India before, so I knew the drill: liquids and dry toast. Yousuf brought a bottle of tonic water (yuk) and tea with three pieces of toast and jam, for energy. I went back to bed for a short while, then moved to the porch to listen to tapes and watch the shikara traffic. One was loaded with Coke, Limka, and mineral water. I didn't ask Yousuf for any of these, as I was almost out of money. I couldn't afford anything until he could take me to an American Express office. This he promised to do the following day, as I also needed to confirm my airline ticket at Air India, for my return to Canada.

That evening, Yousuf brought a beautiful bouquet of gladioli to my room and served omelet and yogurt for my dinner. It was thoughtful of him, but I should have stuck to water as my sleep, what there was of it, was interrupted time and again! I had been alternating between Pethie's (one of my millionaire host's) pills, Pepto Bismol, and water. Had even considered hunting up Dr. Banks' phone number which he gave me in Delhi airport. He said he was going to Srinigar and to give him a call if I needed anything. Well, I certainly did need something, though I don't believe that's what Dr. Banks had in mind!

I felt much better the following day, so the excursion into Srinigar was a welcome relief from sitting on the verandah watching all of the vendors of Kashmiri artifacts pass by. Silver, postcards, papier-mâché--even furs were for sale. Their opening line, as they called from their shikaras: "No need to buy. Only look," had become far too familiar to me now. The Air India building was quite nice, with police and military everywhere. They looked very clean and smartly turned out in their green uniforms. Since Yousuf had been given number 53, I realized we would have lots of time to people watch. Next to me was a beautiful Punjabi lady. She was dressed in yellow and red and was nursing a tiny baby. Her daughter, who was wearing a shocking pink and black flowered dress, was waiting patiently beside her.

Some American tourists were sitting across from me. They appeared to be hippies or possibly trekkers, wearing bummed-out clothes. An older man with a scraggly beard accompanied an English lady, who was wearing an Indian sari and bedraggled scarf to cover her messy hair. Trekkers? Maybe. A young Indian girl, with a bright red bindi on her forehead, was waiting with her boyfriend/husband. They were dressed in blue jeans and Western-style T-shirts and had an expensive camera, so likely had lots of money. Finally, Yousuf returned with bad news. The computers were down! He still had his number, but we'd have to return later. Plan B was for Yousuf to check in at his office. In Travel was on a back street, so that's where I waited with his driver. How long would he be? I had no idea. My former experience with Indian administrators and their love of putting officious-looking stamps on everything was old hat to me. People- watching again…why not? An old man in brown Kashmiri long cape over tan undershirt and pants, with a very long white beard and little cotton Muslim cap, peered in at me. I suppose I looked as foreign to him as he did to me. Next, several brown sheep passed by. Then Yousuf returned. Did I get my money? Yes, though I kept the amount a secret from him. I didn't want him to think I was rich--which I really wasn't!

The following day was the grand excursion to Uncle Abdul's Shaw Art Palace. Okay, it wouldn't really be grand, but you must keep in mind that Madam Barbara was seriously bored! Secondly, it wasn't really a palace--more like a rug emporium. It belonged to Yousuf's uncle. I knew I'd need to be up for some heavy-duty salesmanship. I'd experienced this before, in India. I was taken first to admire the rug crafters at their work. Most were small children learning the trade. Such tedious work, sitting cross-legged before a great expanse of underlay, on which tiny knot after tiny knot was applied to form the pattern. One was a small pure silk (or as the Muslims pronounced it, "silik") rug like the one I had purchased in '82. It was said to have 700 knots per square inch!

Next stop was the showroom, and all master salesmen were on hand to employ their best lines designed to hook the customer. Yousuf's Uncle Abdul Shaw had his employees rushing about unfurling each rug so I might admire its wonderful design and craftsmanship. I did want at least two rugs for myself, but they didn't know that. The presentation was essentially so I might tout this establishment as the best place for the groups I was bringing in the future. Little did we know then, as I said at the beginning of my story, that all hell was about to break out and tourists would not be coming to Kashmir for a very long time.

My eldest son was going to be married when I returned so I bought a small all-wool carpet for him, a similar one for myself, in brown tones, and a larger one, wool and silik, for myself. They were to be sent by air mail to Toronto Airport. Although they were fully insured, I guess I was taking a chance on ever seeing them again! I duly signed my name and purchase code on each rug. Uncle Abdul was apparently pleased with the sale as he presented me with a lovely hand- worked tablecloth worth $300 Canadian.

The next morning my diary read: "Five a.m. and I am feeling so much better! Thank God or Allah, since I am within range of the prayers being said at the mosque nearby. I really was better, and looking forward to going for dinner with Yousuf that night. He had suggested Chinese. Again with the Chinese! I wanted Western. By now I could hardly recall what it tasted like. Although all I had eaten/drunk that day were two Cokes, one Limka, three pieces of toast, and three cups of tea, I don't suppose it mattered where we went. I'd have to be careful, though.

Yousuf tried to get reservations at the Centaur but they were full. It would have to be the next night. I settled for chicken, plain rice, and tea aboard Arizona. It was just as well we didn't go, as a shikara ride that night would have been quite cool. The reader may once again question my judgment--going alone with Yousuf and the Shikara driver on a rather long boat trip to the hotel and back, late at night. As I said before, Krys was a good friend of Bashir's; she had brought them business before and, by now, I had my Connoisseur Travelplan Enterprises, Incorporated. Once again I sense that you're thinking, "How naïve of you!"

Various hindrances prevented our arrival at the Centaur for dinner, but we finally sat down to eat at about 8:00 p.m. The menu was only Indian or Moghul Tandoori. What? No Chinese. I settled for chicken again, mutton in a Moghul hot pot, yogurt, nan (bread), a bloody Mary, and half a beer. I sense that the reader is not showing any signs of envy! You will recall my defense of Indian men and their adherence to propriety when it came to foreign women. Well, I am about to disavow this former belief. It might have been the whiskey that Yousuf drank, or the moonlight, but advances were made that night. His reply to my rejection was, "You don't like men?" I shook my head in the negative. That's all there was to it. We returned to the houseboat and I went to bed.

Krys and Bashir arrived back in a serious rainstorm and Yousuf's mother prepared special Moghul food in their honor. The chicken tikka and basmati rice were a real treat for the tired trekkers. No plans were made for the next day, as Krys required some leisure time to recover. I can imagine that the word was out--that being the arrival of two Canadian ladies who would be potential customers of Kashmiri souvenirs.

My reasoning for this was the proposed water trek arranged with another of Yousuf's relatives. Ajaz, later to be named "the tablecloth man," showed up with a shikara to take us to visit his two grandmothers. We had gone only a short distance when a pile of tablecloths was revealed and the inveterate salesman began his pitch. We didn't make any final decisions, but Ajaz was pleased that he'd had a chance to display his wares.

We were received everywhere with a very warm welcome. The two grannies, sisters, brothers, uncles, and cousins--forty-eight family members in all--lived in three houses. Some were away at college, but that was a lot of people for three homes! At house number one, we remained in the living room. We were served ice-cold Limka, took video pictures of family members, and allowed them to view themselves on the video. We were shown weaving that used yarn made from the neck feathers of a Ladakh bird, and some other family members who were knitting carpets.

House number two was even nicer. We entered and were immediately introduced to Ajaz's grandmother. She was seated on a lovely rug in the living room. Her dress was typically Muslim, with traditional white lace head covering. Their kitchen had white tiled walls in some areas, plenty of shiny metal cooking utensils,

The Journey Itself

and a refrigerator. We were served our second Limka and enjoyed taking more video. It really was amusing to see Granny, probably seventy years of age or more, with one eye closed, viewing herself on an Olympus video camera. Quite a contrast!

At house number three, we had the same reception--only this time we had Kashmiri tea with lots of cinnamon and cardamom. Here, they displayed several beautiful rugs, one of which took eight months to make. By then it was time for the return trip, in Ajaz's office, and plenty of time for further demonstration of tablecloths, shawls, and rugs. Some were left at Arizona for further consideration overnight. The following day, Yousuf was going to take me to the Moghul Gardens in the afternoon, but Arizona's shikara was not available, so we opted for the sound and light show at Shalimar Gardens. Yousuf's car would not be ready until 8:00, so I contented myself with listening to music and sitting on our verandah. When the prayers began at the mosque, I considered saying some of my own for people at home. Do I hear you saying, "Perhaps you should have said some for yourself?" Not a bad idea. I agree.

The next day we decided to cancel our trip to Srinigar, as there was news of serious unrest. Protesting students were met with military and police--some sort of uprising. I had recollections of being in Tianamen Square, in China, just before the appalling massacre in 1989. As well, Srinigar had imposed curfews, as did neighboring Leh and Ladakh. The storm clouds were gathering--those that would eventually prevent tourists from choosing the former paradise of Kashmir as a favorite destination. I hoped there would be nothing in our newspapers at home, or my family would be worrying about my safety. Mind you, I believe they often were concerned whenever I selected any of the exotic destinations that seemed to be my habit. The evening gave proof of growing concern. All of the lights were turned off at the little gazebo at Nehru Park, where young people liked to gather to drink and have a good time.

It was great having Krys and Bashir back--not just for the camaraderie...the meals were better; there were pre-dinner cocktails, wine with dinner--even a few after dinner drinks. I don't want you to assume that we were slipping into alcoholism or anything like that; we were just relaxing and having some fun. For me, anyway, there hadn't been much fun up to this point! Some nights we just sat up-top and enjoyed the beauty of Kashmir's Heaven on Earth, as history has named it. Sunset on Dal Lake is quite wonderful, but for me--as I said previously, it is the Himalayas clothed in soft blue-grey or grey-green and topped with puffy white clouds that appear as a delicious dessert generously garnished with whipped cream. After dark, twinkling lights on houseboats dotted the edge of Dal Lake and shikaras, also bearing little lights, passed by. As well, an almost inaudible dip of paddles could be heard as they passed our houseboat. All was serene.

One night I asked Yousuf to take me to the Shaw Rug Emporium. I was a bit concerned about the mailing instructions. The shikara arrived, but I was not introduced to the boatman. Apparently Yousuf wished to surprise me for, when we passed by Meena Bazaar, I announced that I'd stayed there on my '82 trip. Yousuf's reply was, "Then you will know our boatman, Madam Barbara." With this, Gulam poked his head around the canopy and grinned. My answer was that I certainly did recall Gulam's kindness in bringing many cups of wonderful Kashmiri tea, with cinnamon and cardamom, to my cabin! I did not describe the night on Meena Bazaar when Gulam had arrived at my room with oil and mustard for a massage for Madam Barbara. It was thoughtful of him, but I declined his offer. Let's just say my intuition set up some red flags that night! Another day Gulam asked if I might bring some jeans and a shirt for him the next time I

The Journey Itself

came. He must have intended them for sale, as he never wore jeans himself--just drawstring pants.

As days went by, more and more bad news was reported. Srinigar was under curfew; some riots had broken out; and a 100-year-old school was burned to the ground the next day. I was relieved that my flight was only a few days away. Krys would not accompany me. She was staying on for another week. She seemed unconcerned, but that's just Krys. Nothing ever seemed to bother her. If you want to travel to faraway places, there is always a heavy price to pay--not only in money but in time, along with all of the frustrations accrued on the way. And doing this alone just adds to the burden. I will spare you the details, but here are a few which might interest you.

During the flight from Srinigar to New Delhi, I was afforded a great view of My Himalayas from the air. An Indian gentleman had the window seat and I was on the aisle. However, the opportunity to film the mountains from the plane was too good to miss. I confess to very rudely pushing my way across to take my shot, but couldn't get the camera lined up. Window seat gentleman very kindly suggested that he could take the empty middle seat. Was I successful? Definitely, and as far as I can tell, the view included K2.

At Amristar we took on passengers and, after takeoff, out came the infamous box lunches. In all of my travels, especially to third world countries, I have never had a good box lunch. The word inedible comes to mind, and it was true again. With the exception of the cheese chips, it was a waste of time to have opened the box.

I didn't expect the New Delhi Park Hotel to be five star--not like the beautiful Taj Hotel, in Agra, on my first trip to India, but it was quite nice: clean, plus air conditioning and a fan. One negative point was that the air conditioner leaked and I had to put towels under it. We must remember, though, that nothing is ever perfect. That first evening I decided to confirm my ticket and go to the bar for some finger food and cold Kingfisher beer. Local beer is always good regardless of what country you're in. I had worn my Punjabi outfit and a young India fellow in the elevator said he liked my Indian outfit. I ate dinner at 9:00 p.m. It had usually been 10:00 p.m. anywhere in India or Kashmir.

An Indian gentleman had been loitering in the dining room and, as I got up to leave, he asked me what time it was. When I responded in English, he hurried on his way. I was suspicious when I saw him again as I got my key at the main desk. I definitely made no eye contact, so I was further alarmed when he appeared once more as I entered the elevator. Could he be a stalker? The light was already pressed for the fourth floor, so I just waited. Surprise, surprise; he exited at my floor. I was still maintaining avoidance; I walked right to my door and tried to open it. Damn it! I was unable to get the door open. He noticed my problem and hurried along to help me. Now he even knew my room number! I was further disturbed to realize that the New Delhi Park didn't have much in the way of security. However, despite my concern, I double locked my door and prepared for bed. It wasn't long before I winked out--or in truth, it may have been passed out! The reader may attribute my effortless entry to dreamland to the Kingfisher beer but, in my defense, I really was exhausted.

The following day I walked up to Connaught Place, where all roads run concentrically in a wheel formation. Radial roads run out from the center--quite unique. This was my shopping destination. Actually I didn't buy too much other than an ankle chain, toe rings, and a silver pendant. Ankle chain and toe rings? Was I going too far with the Indian thing?

The Journey Itself

On flight day I had a 3:00 a.m. wake-up call with transportation to the airport at 3:30 a.m., arrival at the airport by 4:00 a.m., and take-off at 7:50 a.m. We had been delayed one hour, but I was thrilled to have four seats to myself and time to sleep on the eight-hour flight to London. Check-in at Heathrow went quite smoothly, except for the fact that I left the X-ray without waiting until my video camera rolled through. I entirely forgot about it until I had gone into a pre-departure area. A very generous English man noticed my distress and hurried me back to discover the personnel searching my camera to try to discover its owner. I explained that it was mine, showed my ID, and the panic was ended.

As I waited in the boarding lounge, I struck up a conversation with a very friendly Indian man from New York. Peter Paul offered me a drink of Chivas, which I gratefully accepted. With dinner he offered a cognac--another of my favorites. After all, it would have been rude of me to decline his offer...wouldn't it? I always dread the New York thing of going from Kennedy to La Guardia, but my new friend had offered to help me with the transfer. Too good to be true? In fact, it was! We arrived late into Kennedy and cleared customs, but I was missing some Air India form I was supposed to have.

My new Indian friend was still nowhere in sight--so I was on my own after all. I finally found a cart and headed for a bus, which took almost one and a half hours to do its route to the other airport. It was 8:10; we still weren't at Air Canada, and visions of having to stay overnight in New York, with all of the attending details of making arrangements, were tumbling about in my crazed brain! My husband would be meeting my missed flight in Toronto and wondering what had happened. The bus stopped a long way from Air Canada, and there were no carts. I was grateful that one young guy agreed to help me despite his friends calling him a "sucker." I rushed in to discover there were still some people in line but, in my agitated state, I went by them to speak to the agent. I could tell she was displeased, but she courteously announced that the flight didn't go until 8:40 and it was only 8:25. Her assurances that I need not worry and that I would get on were music to my ears.

Two more hours to Toronto, plus two more to Brechinbrae, and I'd be home. Total hours since I left Srinigar: 30! The ill-fated pony trek would be over, but I'd be safe and happy at home--at least until I was once more tempted to travel abroad!

Antarctic Adventure: Sailing to the Bottom of the World

In public school, tales of the exploits of famed Antarctic explorers like Scott, Shackleton, Cook, and Amundson stirred my imagination. Some years later, I taught about their journeys. It was always the same. I was unable to complete the reading of the tragic death of Robert Falcon Scott to my grade five students without shedding a few tears. Had the seed already been sown? Was this the beginning of a desire to travel to the unknown land that had drawn these venturesome men to the bottom of the world, to a place which was named Terra Australis Incognita, better known as Antarctica?

On previous trips, other tour members and I would have discussions of places we had been and future destinations that would be on our "must-do" list--or should I say "hope to do." Even then Antarctica was a dream of mine, though not at the top of any list. Nor was it on a list of places that were "calling me." What were some that did call me? No, not outer space! I doubt if that will ever be on my list, although I have often been accused of being "spaced out." I had already been to Canada's Klondike and Northwest Territories, South America, India and Kashmir, Africa, China, and Tibet...so a poem given to me by a friend was very apropos. It was named "The Land of Beyond"--a poem

ANTARCTIC ADVENTURE: SAILING TO THE BOTTOM OF THE WORLD

written by Robert Service. It absolutely fit my desire to travel the world.

> Thank God there is always a Land of Beyond
> For us who are true to the trail;
> A vision to seek a beckoning peak,
> A fairness that never will fail . . .
>
> Robert Service

So in September of 1992, one of the voices from places that "called me" was heard. A small article appeared in a local newspaper. It described an Antarctic/Patagonia expedition aboard a Canadian icebreaker named MV Northern Ranger. Blyth and Company Travel had organized a number of tours. Each would feature a Canadian dignitary. Prime Minister Pierre Elliot Trudeau would be on the first trip and Dr. David Suzuki on the second. Fortunately, I selected the second with Dr. Suzuki. You will learn why I have said "fortunately" later on.

The price was right--about half of what it had been in 1987, when I retired from teaching. I was well aware that it would not provide the luxuries of a typical cruise ship. After all, the ship was not the main focus of this trip. The destination was! I booked right away. I even selected one of the two single cabins, though later on in my story, you will see that this was not the best idea! I had four months to assemble all of the gear required to visit the highest, windiest, coldest (world record -126 degrees Fahrenheit), and driest place on earth. Yes. You guessed it. I was definitely excited! You may imagine the apprehension I felt when I read a full page article in the *Globe and Mail*. It was just two weeks before my departure but, thankfully I was staying in Toronto at the Chelsea Hotel. And, because we didn't take any newspapers published in Toronto, my husband would have been unaware of what was said in that article.

It was entitled "An Epic Journey--Not the Love Boat" and gave all of the gruesome details.

Following is a quote from that newspaper article: "The MV Northern Ranger, with twelve people aboard, sailed, on December 2, from St. John's Newfoundland on what was to be a 38 day, 8500 nautical mile cruise--an epic journey to many of the natural wonders of the Americas. Mr. McInnes wrote, 'By Christmas it had become more like an epic journey to hell!' One day out the Northern Ranger ran into hurricane-force winds and for five days it was rocked by gusts recorded as high as 80 knots, before the wind gauge blew away. Six-story waves rolled past the little ship as it was swept sideways off its course . . . , Most of the passengers were sick. They couldn't even open doors to look out. Small tables, that hadn't been secured, became projectiles as did anything else that wasn't fastened down."

They finally arrived in Bermuda four days later, four days behind schedule, and spent another four days while repairs were made to the ship. Some of the passengers had banded together to hang the owner of the travel company in effigy, in the ship's lounge, and three of the passengers plus three of the hospitality crew jumped ship! At approximately the same time, I heard two CFRB interviews in which the owner spoke from the Northern Ranger via radio telephone. He, of course, painted a very positive picture, adding that the unexpected weather would preclude stopping at some of the planned destinations. Prime Minister Trudeau gave a brief interview, which was also quite reassuring.

I was determined that the disturbing information I had read in the newspaper and heard on the radio would be concealed from my husband and family. That would be my secret until I returned. Do I hear you saying, "*If* you returned?" I'm not surprised. The fact that I did not back out at this point would give you good reason

ANTARCTIC ADVENTURE: SAILING TO THE BOTTOM OF THE WORLD

to question my judgment. I had, however, passed the point of no return. We were leaving in two weeks. I had purchased all of my gear. My trip was fully paid and cowardice did not constitute a medical reason for canceling. My insurance would not cover me for just backing out for any other reason. However, I gained some reassurance that all would go well, as I would be flying to Ushuaia and missing that first hazardous part of trip number one. Regardless of all of my rationalizing, I was going on the voyage of a lifetime. Another of my travel dreams was about to be fulfilled. There could be no room for second thoughts. I was going, come what may!

A long flight from Toronto via New York brought most of our group of 78 passengers to Buenos Aires, Argentina. Others joined us there. I was soon to discover that my fellow passengers had come from many countries other than Canada and the USA: Finland, Denmark, France, England, Australia, Germany, and Holland were all represented. They had seen ads in their local papers as I had done, and jumped at the chance to be part of such an exciting adventure.

What kind of person would travel to Ushuaia, the southernmost city in the world, at the tip of South America, to board an icebreaker for a voyage to Antarctica? The answer to this question lay in the numerous conversations that I was privileged to have with my fellow passengers throughout the trip. They were, as you might expect, all world travelers: naturalists, trekkers, mountain climbers, sailors, teachers, novelists, environmentalists, ornithologists, screen writers . . . . And they were of every age, from the youngest, a three-year-old boy, to the eldest, an 87- year-old lady.

Admittedly, I had quite a few trips under my belt by 1993, but some of these people outranked me in the category of really venturesome trips. A retired professor from California had climbed Mt. McKinley and was accustomed to kayaking in the ocean. Nan, the 87-year-old lady, had crossed the Sahara Desert with a caravan when she was 83! Many had trekked in the Himalayas as I had done. However, their treks in Nepal and Tibet, outranked my one trek. Some had trekked to Base Camp at Mt. Everest. All of their stories were wild and wonderful and I loved every minute I spent listening to them.

Finally we were about to embark from Ushuaia, Argentina. It is at the tip of South America and is squeezed between dramatic mountain peaks and the blue-green Beagle Channel. Yes, it was named for Charles Darwin's ship the Beagle. We set sail in the late afternoon, in brilliant sunlight--temperature 80 degrees Fahrenheit. The captain predicted a smooth passage through the Beagle Channel, and there were rumors that there had been numerous "easy" Drake Passage crossings. Notice that I have called these "easy" crossings rumors, as the waters of the infamous Drake Passage are reputed to be the roughest seas on earth!

Though I had never endured seasickness, I had prepared myself with numerous preventatives: long-lasting Gravol, Transiderm, patches, and sea bands that are worn around the wrists at critical pressure points. In 1993, doctors did not give them much credit with regard to the prevention of seasickness, but sailors recommended them. I took the Gravol when we boarded. The sea bands could wait until it got rough, and the Transiderm and patches might never be needed.

The following day, February 22, I awakened to discover that we were sailing the Drake. It was a glorious day with full sun and just a few clouds. And there was a nice easy roll to the ship. Passengers could stroll about the decks or visit the bridge, where questions were welcomed by the captain and crew. Some chose to listen to naturalists who were delivering very interesting lectures in the lounge. I was in the lounge complimenting myself on being one of the luckiest women I knew. Who would ever imagine that Barb Brechin, a retired teacher, who had literally not been out of Ontario Canada before the 1970s, was sailing Drake Passage on her way to Antarctica?

The thoughts recorded in my journal that day are eloquent testimony to the excitement I felt. I was wondering what the weather had been like when the earliest explorer, Captain James Cook, first sailed these waters, in 1773. When I was teaching there was very little written about Captain Cook's search for Antarctica. However, as I write this story I have access to Google and have learned that "In 1772 he was commissioned by the Royal Society to search for the hypothetical Terra Australis." Later accounts show that the unlocated continent was called "Terra Australis Incognita."

In fact, I wrote a poem when I returned, with that exact name. No wonder I felt so excited that day, as my self-analysis always seems to indicate that I love to follow in the footsteps of famous explorers. Now I must confess to have spoken too soon, for the Drake was about to live up to its reputation. Less than hour after I had written about the "nice easy roll" of the Northern Ranger, the infamous passage, or perhaps the weather, had other ideas.

The winds increased to 60 miles an hour; the waves rose to 8 feet; and wherever you were on the ship you were harshly rocked by the relentless motion from side to side and from bow to stern. A hurricane or near-hurricane was upon us!

The rule given to us when we boarded--"one hand on the ship at all times"--was now religiously followed by all passengers… those, that is, who were still mobile. The dining area on Deck 2 was quite empty that night, as many seemed to have lost their appetites. Pale ghosts of passengers who had boarded at

The Journey Itself

Ushuaia lay sprawled in chairs in the lounge area. No doubt they had escaped from their cabins, which were shared with one or two other passengers who were laid low or busy throwing up. I counted my lucky stars that I had booked a single cabin. I'll recount later on in my story why going single was not "lucky" at all!

You must forgive me for bragging, but I did not experience one moment of seasickness. It must have been the Gravol or the sea bands or, since I've been on other rough seas, possibly I am not subject to seasickness. I walked about, albeit with great difficulty, climbed up to the bridge to watch the raging sea, even spent ten minutes on a rowing machine located in the library, when I was waiting for dinner. That must have presented a humorous picture, as I wasn't even rowing in the direction that the ship was going! Plus it was a stationary machine, so Barb was going nowhere.

That night the captain and crew were all formally introduced, with the exception of the doctor. Certainly not reassuring. When he finally made an appearance we wondered if he would be able to carry out his duties. He was a very pleasant young man, but his ashen complexion suggested that he too had succumbed to seasickness.

I slept fitfully that night, and even confess to having hung on to the side of my bunk, lest I fall out. The Northern Danger, as passengers who had read the newspaper article had renamed her, was on a really good roll. But was I afraid? I must admit to having had some concerns. Our ship, which was only 72 meters in length, with a displacement of 2340 tonnes and speed of 14 knots, could possibly be overturned. She seemed, shall we say, rather top heavy and therefore vulnerable.

The next day, February 23, we were still battling the storm for a few hours until there was some respite from the wind. The sun came out and I was able to see albatross and petrel from my cabin window. However, it was still far too rough to attempt going out on deck. At this point I decided to stay in my very large cabin and do a bit of reading. I had gone for my meals, though there were very few in the dining area--three or four, I think. And it was still far too rough for me to carry my own tray. Some of the crew did that for me. At breakfast that morning, a lady with blood streaming from her hand had had her bathroom door slam against her fingers, and she was in dire need of some help. The metal rim of the heavy door had given her some serious cuts. I recall saying, "Note to self. Be careful!"

By 11:30 p.m. the wind had gone down considerably and was at our stern, so I was able to visit the bridge. What a beautiful view: out over the bow, midnight-blue water as far as the eye could see; toward our stern, a gorgeous pink sky with delicately shaped clouds; some mere slivers of clouds; others a bit of a puff with streaks running out from them.

I took several sunset shots through the glass which, despite my concern that they would turn out to be failures, turned out rather well. Something that Homer had written in his epic poem *The Odyssey* came into my mind: "The ship came to the limits of the world, to the deep flowing Oceanus . . . shrouded in mist and cloud . . . ." Well, we were definitely at the limits of the world. You can't go much further south than Antarctica.

Early the next day, this announcement came over the PA: "You had better get out on deck. This is what you have come to see." And, there they were, on the port side of the ship, the Shetland Islands, some of the more than 20 islands and islets which lie to the north of the Antarctic Peninsula. The chain stretches about 280 miles from its southernmost point at Smith and Snow Islands up to Elephant and Clarence Islands in the northeast. These islands were the first sighted by Captain William Smith

The Journey Itself

of the brig Williams, in 1819. The cliffs, robed in duo tones of blue and white and crowned with glittering sunlight, stood honor guard for us. It seemed a fitting tribute after our display of bravery, which we had shown conquering the Drake.

Coleridge's words from *The Rime of the Ancient Mariner* sprang to my mind as I stood on the deck.

> "And now there came both mist and snow,
> And it grew wondrous cold:
> And ice, mast-high came floating by,
> As green as emerald."

The beauty of the blue and white scenes was almost indescribable, but I must try. As one of the privileged few who have visited the White Continent, I am obliged to share my experience with you--to explain that Antarctica is not the "nether world" you may have believed it to be. In summer, at least, it is a glittering paradise.

Stephen Pyne wrote in his book *The Ice--A Journey to Antarctica*: "Ice is the beginning of Antarctica and ice is its end." He also commented that it was an earthscape turned into an icescape. He also said that although Antarctica was totally covered with ice during the Ice Age, it now displays a multitude of variations on a theme: ice dome, ice sheet, glacier, shelf ice, pack ice, bergs, bergy bits, growlers, brash ice, and ice chips. Two-thirds of Antarctica is ice. In some areas it is 2.5 miles thick. All but 5% of the world's supply of fresh water (99% of which is frozen) lies in this continent at the end of the world. Up to 10,000 flat-topped icebergs are calved from Antarctica's great freshwater ice sheets each year. Yes, we had arrived at a continent whose surface, in winter, is doubled to more than 30 million square kilometers--a surface well over three times the size of the United States of America, or about the size of Africa.

Antarctic Adventure: Sailing to the Bottom of the World

Sorry I have bored you with all of these statistics, but one must know these to appreciate my thrill at having actually been in this environment, even for a few days. Some records speak of men who, when forced to stay for long periods of time at some of the research stations, began to hallucinate or beg to go home. So let's get back to what I loved about Terra Australis Incognita. Bear witness to a small portion of the poem I wrote while aboard the Northern Ranger.

> We had answered the call of silence
> And now in this mystical land
> Frozen music half fierce, half tender,
> Bewitched and enthralled us;
> We most willingly succumbed
> To its hypnotically, imperious command.
>
> "Terra Australis Incognita"
Barbara Street Brechin © 1993

Because the few days we spent in Antarctica were blessed with brilliant sunlight, my description of this glittering earth jewel may seem a bit over the top. However, as I was to discover two years later in the Northwest Passage, these realms are not just black and white or shades of grey, but often filled with color. There were days when the only words to describe this virtual Nirvana were to say that it was a jeweler's showcase of sapphire, opal, emerald, turquoise, and diamond. Given the presence of sunlight, ice can be a beautiful thing!

Most fascinating and awe-inspiring were the bergs. Tabular bergs hugged the coastline; glacier shelf, ice islands, and ice floes glowed blue in a sea whose colors ranged from a dull green-gray to a dark blue-grey, or tar-black. We were overwhelmed by their majestic size, variety of form, and changing hues. Sometimes a berg's translucent blue and green ice, and its reflective snow, made it into a virtual prism. Occasionally, in ice fog, it was highlighted by shadow, producing a grey outline amidst a white mist. Most exquisite to me was a bluish-white berg shaped by wind and sea. It resembled an enormous modernistic sculpture. One of its interior surfaces had captured a shaft of sunlight. It seemed to be illuminated by a giant spotlight.

On the first day we were to go ashore, all were quite excited. As we stood in a line to board the zodiacs, I was standing behind Dr. Suzuki. When he asked if this was my last continent, my response was a breathless, "Yes, it is. I have been on all of other six!"

Hence the following words in my poem:

> For mine was a hidden yearning;
> My last continent, my lifelong dream,
> Just the thrill of the last frozen frontier,
> Terra Australis Incognita, with its ultimate beauty,
> Beauty in the extreme.

Terra Australis Incognita
Barbara Street Brechin © 1993

Our first shore landing was a harbor appropriately named Paradise Bay. My diary reads, "I set foot on my last continent today at 10:00 a.m.--February 24, 1993. I feel tears springing to my eyes now as I write this in my journal." Yes, and that was just the beginning. The day was filled with emotion. From the moment we entered the zodiacs to the excitement of landing and exploring around the Argentinean research station, Asmirante Brown, and the cruise around the harbor, we were all, to say the least, thrilled. There was one moment of apprehension, though, when the guide said it was a bit risky to go right up to one of the huge icebergs. He warned us that the large bergs sometimes become top heavy and overturn but he thought we could take a chance on this particular berg. Our fear was unwarranted, as we had no problem and I got some great photos.

Do I hear you saying, "But did you see penguins?" Oh yes, we certainly did. I am just getting to that now. When we made our second landing at Port Lockroy we were surrounded by hundreds of penguins. There were Adelie, Gentoo, Chinstrap, Macaroni, and Rock Hoppers. They seemed totally oblivious to our presence, so we were able to sit among them and enjoy their antics. Numerous pairs seemed to be arguing; others travelled about in rows of three or four, like little line dancers in formal attire; Rock Hoppers did just that as they hopped from one rock to another. One female was guarding a chick, which had just hatched too late in the season. It would be unable to leave when the others departed for the ocean at the end of summer. Their winter homes are in the seas around the Antarctic pack ice. We did not see any Emperor penguins as we did not go further south where they are located. Their wintering habits are remarkable and totally different. Before we returned to the Northern Ranger I took off my rubber boots and socks so I could test the Antarctic water. Do I hear you asking, "Why?" Well, I had done the same thing when I was at Tuktoyaktuk, on the Arctic Ocean in 1980, so I felt a certain compulsion to do the same at the other end of the world. Yes, as you would assume, there was no difference. It was just as cold!

So we were off to Deception Island. It is a ring-shaped island located north of the Antarctic Peninsula. Storms had forced us to bypass Deception Island as we sailed south. It was expected that we would be able to land now, as we returned. The island is a fabulous example of a caldera...a volcano, the collapsed summit of which forms an interior basin. The summit probably collapsed in stages and one section sank far enough to allow the sea to flood the interior. The ring of snow-covered hills around the resulting lagoon is the remnants of the volcano's summit crater. They form sheer yellow, black, and red cliffs where pigeons, petrels, and fulmars build their nests in precarious nooks and crannies.

We landed at Whaler's Bay and hiked up to Neptune's window, on the caldera. Our naturalist guides warned us to keep our distance from the fur seals that we saw on the beach. It seems that these seemingly awkward creatures can actually move much quicker than a man. It is impossible to outrun them. Also of interest were some deserted buildings, the remains of a plane that had crashed on the beach many years prior to our landing, and numerous tanks and equipment probably used in the whaling industry. Our guides could not explain the tanks. However, the Chilean and British research stations were destroyed in 1967 and 1969 respectively. It was alleged that they were heavily damaged when high seas and volcanic "bombs" wreaked havoc on Deception Island.

We do know that a number of countries would like to lay claim to parts of Antarctica but an Antarctic Treaty was signed in Washington on December 1, 1959. Twelve countries, whose scientists had been active in and around Antarctica during the Geophysical Year of 1957-58 signed. There are now 50 parties to have signed the accord. "Peaceful purposes only" is the main provision of said treaty.

An unexpected whale sighting caused quite a stir as we sailed for King George Island on the afternoon of February 25. "Humpbacks on the starboard side!" brought passengers out on the main deck, and for about twenty minutes we were entertained by two beautiful humpback whales. The captain followed them so we might be able to observe their amazing display, "blowing" and saluting with flukes high in the air before "sounding." It was truly wonderful to see.

ANTARCTIC ADVENTURE: SAILING TO THE BOTTOM OF THE WORLD

The Polish research station, Arctowski, is located on King George Island. We were received most graciously by the fourteen men who man the station year round. I had, as is my custom, carried Canadian flag pins with me (compliments of our Federal MP, the Honorable Doug Lewis). Wherever I have travelled in the world, I have discovered that Canadians are quite popular and the recipients are always grateful to receive a small memento of our great country.

The reception on the beach, by hundreds of penguins and several elephant seals, was equally pleasant. The beach, numerous collections of whalebone, the penguins, the sea... all seemed like a beautiful painting set against an almost unrealistic background of ice and snow--totally bathed in the wonderfully warm light of the sun just before it set. No photograph could capture that exquisite scene, but some of my slides came close.

Up to this point in my story I have not mentioned one of the main reasons I decided to take this particular trip to Antarctica. Dr. David Suzuki is a world-famous scientist and noted environmentalist. His wife, Dr. Tara Cullis, and their two lovely daughters were our fellow passengers on the wonderful Antarctic adventure. We were so fortunate to have David and Tara speak to us about environmental concerns in many parts of the world. As well, we were privileged to see a video of their twelve-year-old daughter's dynamic speech, which she delivered at the World Summit Conference in Rio de Janeiro in 1992. It is now 21 years since Severn gave that speech but now, at 23 years of age, she still continues to speak to schools, corporations, many conferences, and international meetings.

David's lectures identified the "interdependence of the thirty million species, which weave the thin layer of life enveloping the world." He reminded us, too, of our responsibility. "Our home,

The Journey Itself

Planet Earth, is finite; all life shares its resources and energy from the sun and therefore has limits to growth. For the first time we have touched those limits . . . .When we compromise the air, the water, the soil, and the variety of life, we steal from the endless future to serve the fleeting present." (Dr. David Suzuki-1993) Even our travel company for Antarctica had proposed their adherence to an environmental goal: "Our goal is to minimize the impact of our visit to these areas, taking nothing but pictures and leaving nothing but footprints."

In one of his lectures, Dr. Suzuki said, "Yes, even our presence and the increasing popularity of Antarctica as a destination for many more tourists in the future, threaten the sanctity of this pristine continent. Visitors cannot always be trusted to be environmentally responsible. Permanent stations have already encountered the most serious problem in Antarctica - that of waste disposal. But there is growing support to make the entire continent a permanent ecological park. Were that to happen, Antarctica could signal a newfound humility, self control, and respect for other creatures that share the planet with us." (1993)

At the beginning of my story I had suggested it was a bonus that I had reserved a cabin for one person. Now I must tell you about an incident that negates the wisdom of that choice. Most of the passengers had ended the night in the lounge. I was among them. So at 11:00 p.m. I thought I'd head back to my cabin. Along the way, I decided that I didn't want the day to end. It could be a good idea to just go out on the deck for a short while to breathe in the Antarctic air and contemplate the happenings of the trip so far. Several people stood talking at the inside doors, so I passed by them and exited through the heavy outside door. One hand on the ship at all times, I thought as I passed along the deck on the starboard side. I hadn't been out that long when I thought it best to head back. Imagine my dismay when I discovered that the really heavy outside door with its huge metal handles, in the shape of an X, was closed and tightly sealed. A bit farther, and I saw the windows to the lounge. I'll go there and madly wave my arms, I thought. Someone will see me. There was no one left in the lounge! At this point I was getting really scared! [a.] No one knew I was out on deck. [b.] I did not have a cabin mate to report that I had not come back. And [c.] It was very, very, cold. What to do? What to do? Perhaps, if I go around to the port side, that door will be open. I did so, but that big door was also closed. This is really scary! I thought, and returned to where I had exited onto the deck. Miracle of miracles, someone came out and I jumped in! Safe again, I thought. Thank God or whoever is looking out for me!

The next day the captain thought that it would be prudent to head back to the Drake Passage, as rough weather and heavy seas had been forecast. If we made good time, we would be likely to reach and cross the Drake Passage ahead of the storm. The passage gave us no trouble, but by Saturday morning we had still not reached Cape Horn. We discovered that we could not land on the Chilean side, as we had already had our passports stamped in Argentina. Apparently these two countries are not on very good terms.

Actually, mist and fog prevented any view of Cape Horn, the tip of South America, which had proved to be so hazardous for early explorers such as: Magellan, Drake and Cook.

There was to be one more landing at a sheep estancia (a Spanish term for a large rural estate or ranch) at Tierra del Fuego. Some passengers chose not to go ashore that night, as we would not set out until 9:30 p.m. and most of the trip in the small rubber zodiacs would be after dark. I would later regret that I had not made a similar decision.

Outbound from the Northern Ranger, I noticed that the sea was quite rough; the waves were already splashing up over the sides of our craft and it was growing very dark. We had the little three-year-old girl, who was tied by a rope to the zodiac, in our care. She had been given the name of "soap on a rope" because the same thing was done each time she went ashore. Someone suggested that she and the eight-year-old boy should sit between two adults. Seriously good idea and should have been evident when we set out, I thought.

Following a short walkabout, we were entertained in a large hall. A grand array of desserts was spread out before us: fancy squares, fruit loaves, fresh fruit, cakes, tea, and coffee. It was all very jolly, but I was already contemplating our return trip. The sea could be even rougher; we would be sailing in the pitch black of night; the only light was a tiny beam from a spotlight on our ship to the water below...a long, long, way from the Estancia. I planned to get down to the shore so I could get into the first zodiac to depart. Fortunately I did not get into the first boat, as its motor quit five minutes out and the waves, which had splashed in onto the floor, had caused the water to rise to the passengers' knees. To add to the trauma, they had no bailer! They, of course, could contact the ship for help so zodiac number two, my craft could motor on.

My fear was in marked contrast to the children's squeals of enjoyment as the waves splashed over us. When we had cleared the channel and were heading out into the even rougher open sea, I admit to keeping my head down and clutching onto the heavy straps that crisscrossed the floor of the zodiac. That way I would not be able to see how far we still had to go to our ship. Occasionally, I took a quick peek and still saw the Northern Ranger out there in the darkness, casting a tiny beam of light from its searchlight on the black sea which surrounded it. The light seemed to promise safety...if only we could get there!

Antarctic Adventure: Sailing to the Bottom of the World

A Newfie crew member who was operating our zodiac really cheered me up when he said, "Four minutes in that water and it would be all over, Byes!" My thoughts at this point were, Thanks, Bye; now I feel really good. Thanks for cheering me up! He also suggested that we might have to return to the estancia since we were literally making no headway against the waves. I continued to visualize the safe haven of my warm cabin back on the ship and prayed that this would not be my last journey--ever! Since I am writing this now, in 2013, you must assume that we did reach the ship...shaken, but not too upset after our slightly harrowing trip to the sheep estancia. It turned out that all 70 passengers were returned to the ship with four zodiacs working in relay. As well, the conked-out motor on boat number one had been revived.

As our journey drew to a close, I reflected on my Antarctic adventure. Each unbelievable picture, imprinted in my mind, seemed to return on instant replay. Flashes of exquisite beauty: ice cliffs, ice bergs, ice floes, snow, sky and sea, mist and clouds, penguins, seals, whales, and Antarctic birds . . . . I was able, now, to relate to the experiences of Scott, Shackleton, Amundsen, and all of the explorers who had sought Antarctica and the South Pole. But, above all, I had felt the vulnerability of man in such a frigid, unforgiving environment. My fellow adventurers and I had stood on that great white continent, tiny specks of humanity dwarfed by gigantic cliffs and icebergs. The thought I have so often had, returned: What is man that Thou art mindful of him?

Our ship landed back at Ushuaia on February 28. At this point there was still one more place for us to see. We were afforded some time to explore the southern point of Argentinean Patagonia. We walked the trails of Parco Tierra del Fuego (Land of Fire) and visited "The Museum at the End of the World"-- Museo Territorial.

THE JOURNEY ITSELF

From my poem came these thoughts:
But what above all, had been found in the Land of Beyond
In that otherworldly paradise;
Was it a land where we'd found a bond
Midst glaciers, bergs, and ice?
Was there a bond between us and the spirits
Of men who had sought the Pole;
Or were we, for just an instant, linked to our Creator
And his Omnipotent, Almighty Soul?

Terra Australis Incognita
Barbara Street Brechin © 1993

Yet all experience is an arch wherethro'
Gleams that untravelled world whose margin fades
For ever and ever when I move.

Ulysses
Tennyson,

Wild Exotic Papua New Guinea

The reader may be wondering, "Why would Barb Brechin want to go to Papua New Guinea?" Well, I will tell you how it happened. The island did not really "call me." Nor did I ever learn about it or teach about it at public school. It happened like this. A friend of mine who is in the travel business advertised it in the *Globe and Mail* and coincidentally, my pilot son was returning a plane via Papua New Guinea to Canada. Still not a reason for me to go? You may know by now that I enjoy exotic and unusual travel destinations. That's my one defense for this one! However, there is one more. Perhaps I should add that I had just returned from Antarctica so now, in 1994, a warm exotic country might be just the trip for me.

I knew literally nothing about Papua New Guinea other than the fact that it was north of Australia, and the second largest island in the world. So pre-trip I looked up Wikipedia and "got the lay of the land." Papua is a sovereign island nation located on the eastern half of New Guinea. Since the 19th century it has been known as Melanesia. It is also one of the most unexplored. Now that sounds like my kind of destination. Even the early explorers hadn't found this one! In fact, to quote Emil Nolde, the German expressionist painter, he declared that in the early 1900s "these brown people are in a phase of their development at which the Germans were 2000 years ago." That would have been when

The Journey Itself

the people were still headhunters. Mmm! Perhaps this wasn't for me. Oh well, it was 1994 now, so they should be over that phase. As well, I learned that the Southern Highlands of Papua New Guinea, where we would first land, had just been discovered in 1930. I said to myself, "You'll be all right." That's what my husband always said when I worried about things.

The info I gleaned from my research said that most of the people still lived in traditional societies or clans and practiced subsistence-based agriculture. In fact, the government hoped to keep it that way, with only Papua New Guineans holding land. They plant in October, before the rains begin, and harvest in April or May. Their diet consists primarily of yams, taro, coconut, sugarcane, and bananas. Occasionally they enjoy fish, wild fowl, pork, or sea fowl eggs. There are other foods too numerous to mention, but I feel you would like to know that they chew betel with lime as a popular stimulant.

Next to the chief sorcerer, the garden magician is the most important person in their villages, possibly even more than their chief. This power is handed down in the female line. In some villages, fishermen are organized into detachments, each of which is led by a headman who owns the canoe, performs the magic, and reaps most of the main catch.

I am certain you have had enough of Barb, the teacher, so let's get right to my story. We arrived in the capital, Port Moresby, with just a quick stop before we boarded a light airplane to fly us into the Southern Highlands for a grassy landing. Yes, that was their landing strip. The people who greeted our tour leader were quite friendly, so no need to hang onto our heads here! Our hotel was what you would expect in this location - wooden construction but quite acceptable. Back in 1930, the aboriginals thought that the white men who had found them, were ghosts of their ancestors and that they had returned from some Spirit World bearing cargo for them. Some even thought that Europeans had intercepted cargo which should have been theirs.

One thing I knew was that no one was getting my new Pentax camera! With the advent of missionaries, New Guineans readily accepted the Bible, believing it to provide some sort of magic which would endow them with the things they desired. One of their wise men thought the foreigners had torn the first page out of the Bible - the page that said that God was actually a Papuan.

You may ask why Stone Age Man was so unaffected by the Jet Age, why so remote, so wild, so unchanged by the rest of the world. The answer lies in the dramatic geography of Papua New Guinea. Rugged mountains form the central spine of the island; mighty rivers rush or meander through jungles and dense rain forests; ravines plunge; spectacular coral reefs lie adjacent to tropical islands, and mangrove swamps fringe the coast. Add to this the heat and humidity of an island just south of the equator and you will realize how forbidding it must have been to early explorers.

Even today, travel between the south and north coasts of PNG still means flying in a small aircraft to the remote Southern Highlands. However, for cruises (the best way to explore the Sepik River and its tributaries or to sail along the Trobriand Islands) modern-day tourists travel in air conditioned ships such as the one we took: The Melanesian Discoverer. For while I enjoy traveling to exotic destinations, I have never embraced the type of loose travel that *Lonely Planet* describes as involving a dugout canoe. That would be too loose for me!

The Melanesian Discoverer provided comfortable cabins, good food, safe drinking water, and informational briefings, as well as shore excursions via jet boat or zodiac, an expert crew, and experienced guides. We could always return to the comfort of air conditioning and a haven from the pesky mosquitoes.

Before we arrived in Papua New Guinea we were advised that since tourism here was still in its infancy--the last twenty years (in 1994)--we who were privileged to travel to this destination should respect the environment and, more particularly, the culture of these primitive people. For this reason our ship had been specifically designed not to pollute the river, and not to leave a huge wake that could endanger the people in canoes or cause danger to the riverbanks.

The last great phase of exploration had occurred in the Southern Highlands in the 1930s. I am describing what I observed in 1994. More could have occurred by this time - 2013. Quaint village hamlets were surrounded by dense rain forests, which were a sanctuary for a very prolific bird population, including a variety of the famous Bird of Paradise. One of our tour members had come to PNG specifically to get a sighting of these magnificent birds.

Papua New Guineans are not only separated from the outside world, but from each other, by peaked mountains and swiftly flowing rivers. For this reason, many tribes have their own district language. Actually there exist more than 740 languages--a third of all languages in the world. Some have learned to speak Pidgin English. Interesting phrases such as: "Something has gone bagarap" (is broken), "Mix master belongem Jesus Christ" (helicopter), and "Nambawan Son belongem Misus Kwin" (Prince Charles) were translated with amusement.

Most New Guineans are subsistence farmers. They practice gardening skills that go back 9000 years. Pigs are highly prized commodities, which are valued as a "bride price" payment--20 pigs plus K600 (more than $600 US) in the Highlands. We saw

Wild Exotic Papua New Guinea

a woman "rota tilling" her garden with a pig tied to the end of a long rope. PNG version of "pig on a rope," no doubt!

Sing-sings may be held for any number of reasons: paying off a bride price, a moga ceremony, a harvest festival or, as we were about to find out, to entertain tourists. Our first of many was held for us in the village of the Southern Highlands. We were allowed to watch their preparations as the clansmen, and one bare-breasted woman, painted their faces and bodies, adorned themselves in cassowary plumes, kina shells, dog tooth necklaces, bark belts, arm bands, aromatic leaves, and grass skirts. The colors--red, yellow, bright green, black, white, and grey--transformed their appearance. They seemed brighter and more colorful than the parrots or their famous Birds of Paradise.

Sepik River Experience: The mighty ever-changing Sepik River runs 1126 kilometers from its source, in the central mountains, to the sea. The most artistic villages are concentrated in the central Sepik, and the most spectacular scenery is on the lakes and tributaries. There are numerous different language groups and clans whose lives depend on the river as a trade route. In most cases each village possesses its own unique character, architectural style of homes, Haus Tambaran (spirit house), artifacts and sing-sings. They believe that the spirits live within these houses, so the carvings that represent them will be found within the building. The spirit houses are off-limits to women (tourists excepted). Another rather gruesome tradition is that each young man must perform a ritual when he comes of age. His initiation includes his requirement to kill someone to acquire a skull to put beneath every post of the Haus Tambaran.

The initiation also required these young men to perform at a flute ceremony wearing what was called a penis gourd. I can imagine that the thing to do was boast about the length of their penises, but I had already taken the picture when I realized there could be no way the penis would have filled those huge gourds! When I had my film developed all I could say was, "Really!"

Our expeditionary cruise along the Sepik River brought us from the Melanesian Discoverer, by speedboat, into many of the villages. What a privilege it was to be granted this intimate experience. As I had expected, the real fascination of Papua New Guinea was its people--the men and women, of course; however, my favorites were the beautiful children, many of whom were festively dressed so that they might participate with their elders as they entertained the foreigners with their sing-sings (dancing and singing, plus drums and flutes. They captured my heart.

We found the most fascinating form of art and craft work in PNG--possibly the world--in the Sepik region. It was indeed a mecca for art connoisseurs...and for this literally untouched society, a vital part of their economy. Their traditional creation of masks has more than one purpose. Yes, they love to dress up in these for festive occasions, and they sell some to interested tourists; but this craft provides a spiritual link with their past. In fact, they once held the belief, and probably still do, that the spirits of their ancestors reside in the masks.

At Tambanum Village, Jan translated that one of the craftsmen would like to paint the face of one of our tour members. As was my custom, I volunteered. Three of my alleged friends offered to stand by as I lay, eyes closed, on a raised platform while the artist executed his skill. I use the word "executed" with a slight bit of trepidation. Okay, it was 1900 when they were still head hunters, and this was 1994. Yet, I had seen one of the young men wearing a T-shirt that read: "Send more tourists. The last ones were delicious!" Obviously, some foreigner thought this was a great joke and the villager likely didn't know what it said. Undoubtedly, there was no danger to me. The artist just hoped to sell a mask. It took quite a while, and when I called out to my friends, there was no answer. They were there, all right, but thought they would tease me by not answering. Children's little brown faces were peering down at me and the mosquitoes were getting their fill of my blood. Regardless of all this, I doubted that I was really in any danger.

To my surprise, the experience was unbelievably pleasant, verging on spiritual. I lay beneath the shade of the roof with a light breeze blowing across my face. Considerate villagers brushed away the pesky "nat nats" (mosquitoes). I just closed my eyes and gave way to the moment. Was it just my imagination, or did I actually see an ancestral face behind my closed eyes? The mask, colors and design, were an amazing reproduction of the New Zealand Maori headband I was wearing, as well as some of the design on my T-shirt. A journalist who was traveling with us used a picture of me with my face painted, holding the mask, for his newspaper's (*Experience Sepik*) front page. I knew the artist hoped to sell me the mask, but I had to disappoint him. It was far too large to transport to Canada.

Our visit to the Murik Lakes was to provide an unexpected experience for me. We travelled by speedboat along the exciting waterway, skimming below the overhanging jungle growth as the egrets rose hastily ahead of us and a few crocodiles checked us out! Then we proceeded to the mangrove-lined lakes and for an Easter Sunday visit to the village of Mendam. The presentation here was not a sing-sing, but a delightful little drama performed my some young Papua New Guinean actors. Following this, I presented Canadian flag pins and colorful postcards of Canadian scenes. The head man of the village did not speak English, but seemed very pleased. Our departure was delayed as one of the young actors came running to get his postcard signed. And as I moved to my seat at the back of the boat, the head man, or perhaps chief, was calling, "Wait, wait!" He came onto the boat, strode down to me and, with arms outstretched, presented the most masterfully carved walking stick. It was too wonderful for words. The dark wooden stick was intricately carved with four masks back and front of the piece of artwork. I have rarely been as thrilled to receive such a gift as I was that day in this primitive society. I was able to walk through customs with no questions asked, as I was using it to aid my walking. How did those people know I was already suffering from fairly serious arthritis? Must have been spiritual intuition.

Trobriand Island Cruise: For seven days we cruised among a myriad of superb islands, islets and atolls of the Siassi Amphlett, D'Entrecasteaux, and Marshall Islands. These islands are set in the tail of the great islands of New Guinea with the Trobriand Group lying splayed out beyond the tail like glittering gems in a coral sea. We thrilled to the many colors of these tropical seas: aquamarine, turquoise, cobalt, sapphire, amethyst, midnight blue . . . It was a kaleidoscope of glittering white sandy beaches, emerald green of lush foliage, dark charcoal-grey of the ridges and sheer cliffs, and the corals and brilliant reds of exquisite sunsets. Sigh! Never to be forgotten!

Sing-sings, performed on the beaches, featured beautiful young bare-breasted girls in grass skirts, though young men and boys often joined in. These delightful people seemed more Polynesian than Melanesian. In contrast to the Sepik villages, the people in these islands seemed to rely more on the sea. However, the cultivation of yams is central to their culture. In fact, it has become a cult, with accompanying rituals such as festivals and filling of yam houses for each wife.

During the sing-sing at Banadi, a torrential downpour forced us to seek shelter in the church/school. We sat on the ground as they sang their songs, and then we were asked to sing. They had ended with their national anthem, so we regaled them with "O Canada" and ridiculous renderings of "Row, Row, Row Your

Boat" and "Old Mac Donald." Sitting there among these friendly villagers, it was hard to believe that they were head hunters as recently as 1900.

At the end of our cruise, our new friend, Jan, sent us on our way with "Lukem Yu Behaen!" We didn't promise to abide by her wishes--partly because, at first, we didn't understand; and partly because it's rather hard for inveterate travelers to make such a promise. One thing we would never forget is that another travel dream had been fulfilled and that memories of Wild Exotic Papua New Guinea were indelibly etched in our memories.

I didn't know it then, but in the years that followed I would realize many more dreams of travel. They say you make your own luck. Maybe, but few are allowed to fulfill as many travel dreams as I have!

The Elusive Northwest Passage

Someone once said that travel is a dream and the person who turns that dream into a reality is indeed a happy person. I know this to be true, for many of my travel dreams have already been realized. Yet my dreams still continue.

> Ever a still small voice calls me;
> Whispers softly in my mind;
> Year after year it continues
> Until at last I find . . .
> Though dream after dream is realized
> I am called to another "Land of Beyond"
> For these are the lands that call me
> These are the ones of which I am fond.
>
> Barbara Street Brechin '95

It's 2013 now, but these memories are still as clear today as they were just after this exciting trip in 1995. I had just returned from an Antarctic adventure with David Suzuki when, out of the blue, a chance to sail the entire Northwest Passage beckoned me. The seed of experiencing this adventure, sown in childhood, begged to be nourished and to bear fruit. Unable to resist, I booked a Marine Expedition journey which would, if I was fortunate, carry me from Greenland, through the Northwest Passage to the Beaufort Sea, in the western Arctic.

I could never forget the words of Stan Rogers' famous song, which reflected my own desire to complete the Northwest Passage, all the way from Greenland to the Beaufort Sea. Stan Rogers' words played and replayed in my mind. My heart sang with anticipation. Yes! Yes! If all goes well, soon the elusive passage will be mine!

Descriptions of this part of the world abound. Milton wrote of a passage where: mountains of ice lay--mountains that stopped the imagined way beyond Petsora, eastward to the rich Cathian coast. Pytheas called it, "Ultima Thule" -- the utmost bound of the earth , where the sea is covered with a strange substance so that it can neither be traversed on foot nor by boat; and, just beyond Thule, it is congealed."

Pliny called it, "Mare Concretum-- the Concrete Sea."

My travel dream this time was filled with the expected: enormous spreading vistas, bleak, stark, and white, great expanses of sky, icebergs, ice floes, birds, mammals . . . Landmarks along the route, where Arctic heroes such as James Cook (1728 - 1779), Sir Alexander Mackenzie, (1789), Sir John Ross(1818), Sir William Edward Parry (1819-1820), Sir John Franklin (1819-1822) and others who fought their way through unforgiving ice, would help me to have some insight into their awful struggles to gain the Passage.

Roald Amundsen made the first successful transit in 1906. It was my hope to do as he had done. What a thrill it would be to sail the entire passage and reach the Beaufort Sea! However, in so doing I dared to presume that I might quaff ambrosia from Pierre Berton's Arctic Grail and to quench my thirst for beauty

The Journey Itself

and excitement, which I had experienced at the other end of the world, in Antarctica. Following is my account of yet another attempt to fulfill a dream of travel.

Nothing could have prepared me for, in the words of Edgar Alan Poe, "this dream within a dream". I could never have anticipated the emotions which would be stirred within me as I experienced the compelling grandeur that lies in Canada's High Arctic--the beauty, the size of the icebergs, the color . . . . Nor did I ever expect to meet two modern-day heroes: Laurie Dexter and Vello (unknown last name) of whom I will speak later in this memoir.

In his book *Arctic Dream*, Barry Lopez describes the popular concept held by southern cultures: a wasteland of frozen mountains, of violent winds, and incipient evil. Seventh-century theologians described it as a place of spiritual havoc--the abode of Antichrist. I am certain that, given the wrong time of year, and less than favorable conditions, our little band of adventurers would have been forced to concur with either or both of these.

In one of his lectures, Laurie Dexter spoke of the expected awful emptiness, which is the traditional view held by outsiders; yet he prepared us, if we were willing, to experience the awesome fullness that aboriginal people know to be a fact of life in the High Arctic. I must, if possible, beam you up to another dimension, one where tiny people in miniature zodiacs are surrounded and dwarfed by leviathan icebergs. Some are as long as a football field and perhaps twenty feet high. In addition to this, you must know that two-thirds of these giants are below water. You must stand with me on the bow of our ship, gasping as rosy sunsets explode in the evening sky. You will then be encouraged to stare in disbelief at vistas filled with charcoal mountains set against the lilac clouds that hang in a pale blue sky, just as the sun disappears from sight.

The Elusive Northwest Passage

We will be enchanted by seascapes and landscapes painted with exquisite color that must be experienced to be believed! Immense cliffs, home to hundreds of thousands of birds, will rise above our zodiacs. Mountains, icebergs, bergy bits, glaciers, and straits choked with ice . . . all of these and more will cause me to repeat what I have so often felt during my travels: "What is man that Thou art mindful of him?"

To expand that thought further, I offer this. What I had expected to be a rather ordinary photo of a sunset--a bright blue sky with some clouds, a golden horizon, and a red-black sea--when developed, revealed a soft black cloud shaped like an arm reaching down so that the hand just touched the water where the sky shone the brightest. Coincidence? I think not. I choose to believe that it symbolized the Hand of God!

But I digress. If you are to share my excitement, experience the fulfillment of my dream, and understand the dream within the dream, I must begin at the beginning. In August, aboard an Estonian research vessel, The Livonia, we set sail from Sondre Stromfjord, in Greenland, and headed for Ilulisaat (a place by the icebergs). Ilulisaat, aptly named as the world's most active glacier, is located here. It moves between 25 to 30 meters a day, calving across a front 10 km in width. This is the origin of most of the Arctic icebergs. It releases some 15,000 sizable bergs each year. Two-thirds fragment and melt away. The rest make their way south, melting and shredding bergy bits as they go.

From the west coast of Greenland they head north across Baffin Bay; then they begin a long drift south to Labrador, Newfoundland, and the North Atlantic. Our first encounter was in the iceberg-filled fjord known as Disko Bay, 180 miles above the Arctic Circle. From our miniature zodiacs, we arched our necks to look "way up". Friendly giants? Yes, or so they seemed. However, we had been warned by Laurie that life in the Arctic is

The Journey Itself

uncertain at the best of times--and unforgiving at others. It was with some apprehension then that we drew close to them.

Consider these statistics. Some are 200 feet high and 1200 feet long. The mariner's rule considers that 4/5 of its height 7/8 of its mass lies beneath the water. Would you trust yourself totally to the whim of these potentially malevolent monsters? I think not. Those who venture among these bergs would do well to abide by the Greenlandic word imaq'a (perhaps) as their cautionary byword. We enthusiastically agreed.

To do justice to the colors of Arctic icebergs an artist would require a broad palette, one that would enable him to paint the soft golden-white glow of early morning when the sunlight spotlights bergy bits floating in blue-black water, the crisp blinding white of midday, the alabaster sides and pearl-colored tops of immense icebergs beneath an overcast sky, the sapphire-blue of those resplendent in a gentian sea, set against an apricot horizon bedecked with lilac clouds, or the reddish-yellow of twilight when the ice takes on the colors of the sun and even the water is tinged with red. Sorry--I really did get carried away there... just as I did in real time!

We had easy sailing across Davis Strait, though it was scattered with icebergs of slightly smaller dimension. The Davis Strait sea ice was cause for little concern, though our captain had to avail himself of radar to avoid the middle pack, which might have been a problem. With two days at sea we were able to enjoy some of Laurie Dexter's lectures aboard the Livonia. He shared the great wealth of knowledge he had gained about the High Arctic: culture of the people who lived there, their language, and ice geography. He inspired us with stories and slides of his exciting career. Laurie was one of the two Canadians who was part of the Polar Bridge ski adventure. He and a group of Russians skied from Siberia across the North Pole to land on

The Elusive Northwest Passage

Ellesmere Island-- Canada's third-largest and most northerly island. As well, his Antarctic adventures and trips to the South Pole were riveting.

We entered sun-drenched Pond Inlet early in the morning. Pond Inlet, on the northeast coast of Baffin Island, is one of the most attractive settlements in the Arctic. Much of the beauty here may be attributed to a range of glacier-crowned mountains, with an ice cap that is over 4000 feet above sea level. This ideal setting was selected first by whalers in the 1800s. Then came the Hudson Bay Company and RCMP. When I was there in 1995 we found a very modern community. No, they don't live in igloos! This was our first encounter with people of the High Arctic. In fact, throughout the entire voyage we visited only three communities: Pond Inlet, Holman, and Cambridge Bay. We were to discover the warmth and friendship of the people of each of these isolated communities in the far north.

I believe it was at Pond Inlet that a small number of schoolchildren convinced one of our guides to take them back to our ship for a short visit. They were so excited that Geoff took them in the first zodiac. By the time we got there, they were running here and there on the ship, investigating the cabins and offices. Some had even helped themselves to pens in one office. I can imagine that Geoff was not surprised, as he did not chastise them for that.

Our journey continued on to Bylot Island, which is one of the favored nesting places for the migratory birds of the Eastern Arctic. The cliffs here provide summer homes and hatching grounds for rare peregrine falcons and ivory gulls, as well as thousands of murres, kittiwakes (at Button Point on the southeastern shore), and snow geese. Canada is home to a major part of the world's snow goose population. More proof of the awesome fullness that I had not expected to see in the High Arctic.

The Journey Itself

This island had been designated as a migratory bird sanctuary and was, in 1995, part of the proposed North Baffin Island Park. In what I called The Great Bird Escapade, we became part of a Hitchcock experience. Before this trip, I had no idea how numerous the bird population was in the Arctic. Thousands of birds: Northern fulmars, kittiwakes, black guillemots, glaucous gulls, thick-billed murres...47 species in all during the complete voyage. Some of these were to be found here on the immense cliffs that rise ledge upon ledge, thousands of feet in the air. We witnessed their aerial performances and marveled at the compelling if not fearsome noise.

Bylot Islands peaks rise 4000-5000 feet with their ice-cap domes on top reaching to 6000 feet above sea level. Small wonder, then, that we were within sight of the Sermilik Glacier for much of the afternoon's cruise. The huge dimensions of the landscape were the primary cause of our inability to judge distance, so for a long time that sunny afternoon our ship seemed almost there. When I had my slides developed, I was grateful for this, as some of the most magnificent exposures were a result of this time span. We saw the rich mahogany-brown and puce of shoreline, the mauve-white of the glacier mouth receding to the stark white of the mountain and the ice-cap dome. Flanked on either side were the Indigo Mountains. All of this lay beneath a powder-blue sky with a few amethyst clouds! What can I say if not to ponder once more that this can only be a dream within a dream.

Our party landed and began what proved to be a very challenging hike for the most adventurous among us. Some of our group followed the circuitous route over the glacier's deposit--a terrain which, I confess, was beyond my physical capability. Several guides carried huge rifles just in case any wildlife should show up and, although the edge of the glacier seemed quite near to them, they finally disappeared from our sight. Upon their return

The Elusive Northwest Passage

we went back to the Livonia and proceeded through Lancaster Sound to Prince Leopold Island. A foreshadowing of what lay ahead could be sensed in the bitter cold winds and increasing number of ice floes that lay in our way. However, we were able to set this aside in order to once again marvel at the grandeur of the bird cliffs. Over 360,000 seabirds came to breed here in the 1970s, and 55 species were recorded on the island. Gigantic ice sculptures loomed above our tiny zodiacs, but a fortuitous wind pushed the ice floes away. Brilliant sunlight sparkled on the water and, once again, all was right with our Arctic world! Somerset Island, also known as Port Leopold, is the location of an old Hudson Bay post. It was here that we strolled amid the ruins and tried to imagine what it must have been like for James Clark Ross and his men to winter over. Scary words for those brave men who had come unprepared into a world much different than jolly old England. History records that they were wearing blue serge overcoats and clothing unsuitable for Arctic weather.

My diary for August 27, recorded that I had been standing on the bridge at 11:00 p.m. with the words of Stan Rogers'song repeating and repeating in my mind. His song outlined the same desire I had. It was to sail the Northwest Pssage to the Beaufort Sea. And further on in my notes: "What a fortunate lady to be living my dream aboard the Livonia!" I could not have known then that the romanticism of that moment would soon be challenged by our experience following the landing at Beechey Island and beyond!

Our Beechey Island experience was very interesting. This island is sometimes compared to Gibraltar, as it stands at the crossroads to the Arctic. Wellington Channel lies north; to the west Is Barrow Strait; to the east is Lancaster Sound; and to the south, Prince Regent Inlet and Peel Sound. Sir John Franklin and his men wintered over at Beechey and there had always

The Journey Itself

been much speculation as to why no message had been left here in a cairn. Was he so certain of "getting through" that year? Was it because the two ships were driven involuntarily away from Beechey Island, along with the ice, in a sudden spring gale, before he could prepare a record? Or was there a message left that was never found?

What we did find on Beechey Island were graves and weathered headboards that marked the last resting place for four of Franklin's men. By 1995 there had been new headstones placed in front of those, with the dates of death. I heard later that the men died of lead poisoning. It seems that the English were just beginning to put food in cans and used lead to seal the cans. The Breadalbane, which had gone in search of Franklin and his men, sank here in 340 feet of water off Beechey Island. It was found by Canadian divers who were part of a National Geographic team in 1981. This expedition was of particular interest to me, as my son had flown supplies there, from Resolute Bay, where he was stationed. John was present when they raised the ship's wheel.

As I sat on the rock beside the graves, with the wind sweeping across the dark water and howling up the cliffs above, I was able to confirm the words of Roger's song. I had seen "the hand of Franklin reaching for the Beaufort Sea." Then the present seemed to fade and I was able to commune with the spirits of those brave men. They had lived and died in that world "so wild and savage." If you should wish to learn much more about these men and the details of the discoveries made by Owen Beattie and his research team, I advise you to read *Frozen in Time— Unlocking the Secrets of the Franklin Expedition.*

In the 1980s, they exhumed the bodies of the men who were buried in the graves. Owing to the weather at Beechey Island, the bodies of Thomas Morgan, William Braine, and John Torrington had been "frozen in time." The results of the autopsies showed that the causes of the deaths were undoubtedly pneumonia, tuberculosis, and /or lead poisoning. The British had just begun to can food at that time and the cans had been sealed with lead! I pondered whether these three young men would have considered the risk taken to be worth losing their lives. And, as to the men who sailed on, a document was found at Victory Point written May 28, 1847. It read, "All well!" Little did they realize that, in the end, all would be lost.

We returned to our ship just in time. Ice blew in and completely clogged up Terror Bay and Erebus Bay. We were about to learn how powerful and terrifying Arctic ice can be! Barrow Strait tried desperately to hold us as the Livonia struggled through 10/10 multi-year ice to Peel Sound. However, it was finally evident that we were stuck in the ice. A call went out to Canada's coast guard and we were assured that help would be on its way.

We awaited the arrival of the Henry Larsen for what seemed like an eternity. As we stood on the deck, in the early morning of the following day, a tiny speck appeared on the horizon. It had to be our savior and a cheer went up from all who were anxiously waiting. Then, when she began her task of freeing us, the Henry Larsen was wonderful to watch. I spent hours on my knees watching. No, I wasn't praying. If we wanted to be on the bridge, it was compulsory for us to keep down so the captain and all could see what was necessary for them to do in concert with the Larsen. It was fascinating to see the stern of the coast guard ship dip down into the sea with a bang and then raft up on the ice time and time again to break our path.

Vello, one of the crew on the Livonia, was very shy and unassuming. However, none of these attributes were apparent when he delivered some very interesting lectures. He had taken part in the building of our ship and he was an important person in all research of the physics required to do this. However, the KGB accused him of being a spy. This resulted in a dedicated scrutiny of himself, his family, and some of his colleagues, followed by a ten year imprisonment. Vello had spent time in Antarctica rock climbing, so he had much to tell about that. My memory of another attribute which Vello possessed is uncertain--but I believe it was heroism. Apparently he saved a number of men during a fire at an Antarctic research station and received an award from his country for this. Our guide, Laurie Dexter, said he could think of no one he'd rather have backing him up than Vello.

It was during our landing on the shores of Kakyoktok River that Vello was to distinguish himself once more. This landing typified the true Arctic paradise, which one could only hope to experience: spongy tundra, alive with Arctic flora and fauna, caribou, Canada geese, tundra swans, a golden eagle, some old Inuit stone caches, and musk oxen.

All of this was wonderful to see, but it was the musk oxen that stole the show--a display expertly captured on video by Vello. We had the rare chance to watch these almost prehistoric animals as they grazed by the water's edge. Then we climbed much higher, but were able to descend to within camera range and take a number of excellent photos before they sensed our presence. Vello, who had positioned himself behind some rocks, caught the action of these magnificent animals as they fled from us. Were we in any danger? Was Vello? Suffice it to say that this exhibition of their power--the thundering hooves, the speed of their flight--was humbling, and we were thankful that we had not come between them and the water. But we were never in any real danger. Nor was Vello.

I must confess that, despite the feeling of privilege in being a member of this expedition, there was an underlying hint of apprehension and fear on several occasions. Things can always go wrong. Yet the excitement and anticipation commingled with these aspects of our voyage to exhilarate us to unexpected highs! Shortly after our zodiac landing at Jenny Lind Island, the ground was blanketed with snow and an ominous fog rolled in. The USA had maintained a base here as part of the Early Warning Dew Line System during the Cold War. We all contemplated the isolation that must have been experienced by those who were posted there. We were indeed grateful to return to the Livonia for a hot lunch and our comfortable accommodation aboard the ship.

The northern community of Holman, on the western shores of Victoria Island, gave us a very warm welcome. To quote one of our tour leaders, Geoff Green, "From the moment we landed on the snow-covered beach and were swarmed by dozens of excited children, to the last zodiac departing for the ship, we experienced the friendliness and genuine hospitality of these Inuit people." We were given a tour of the community and a chance to purchase some of their art, for which Holman is famous. Then it was on to the school gymnasium for a fantastic performance of Inuit music and dance, including their ancient drum dance, plus throat singing and a demonstration of some of their games.

Before we flew to Yellowknife, we landed at Cambridge Bay, on Victoria Island. A delightful young teen gave us a tour of her home village. Naturally she was proud of most of the history of Cambridge Bay, but did not spare us the distressing details of teenage addiction to alcohol and drugs. Most of us are aware of this, but do not realize the distress and cataclysmic effect these addictions have on the youth of high Arctic communities such as Cambridge Bay. Our young guide said that there were several sources of help available now, but that some of the afflicted teens were already beyond asking for help!

Our flight from Cambridge Bay stopped briefly at Yellowknife; then it was on to Edmonton, where a flight to Toronto would bring an end to our Northwest Passage Adventure. I hope the reader can sense the great satisfaction and sense of accomplishment that I felt, and still feel now, in receiving a Northwest Passage Chapter Certificate that states: "Bear witness that Barbara Brechin, having demonstrated the initiative, integrity and bold adventurous spirit of the original Northwest Passage explorers, will hereafter be recognized as an honorable member of the exclusive Northwest Passage Chapter, Order of Arctic Adventurers."

Seeking His Holiness the Dalai Lama

It had been only three years since I had returned from my ill-fated pony trek in the Himalayas, and thankfully most of the anxiety I had experienced during that ridiculous adventure had faded. So, when Krys suggested another India trip, the inveterate traveler--make that travel addict-- agreed. Her proposal this time was that we would make an attempt to meet the renowned Dalai Lama, whose home is in Dharamsala, India, in the foothills of the Himalayas. Prior to my 1985 journey to Tibet, I literally knew nothing about the Dalai Lama. I realized he had been a Nobel prize winner, and was the spiritual and political leader of the country "on the roof of the world" but, other than that, practically nothing.

On that trip I was to discover that, to his people, he was their God King. Tibetans were known to travel hundreds of miles until they reached Lhasa; then, circumambulating (moving the width of their body, prostrating themselves on the ground, getting up and repeating this), they would reach the Temples and the Palaces of His Holiness the Dalai Lama. Everywhere we went, his people would run after us shouting, "Dalai Lama! Dalai Lama!" I was to learn later that they hoped tourists would have a picture of him that they could carry back to their homes.

The Journey Itself

Everywhere we visited--the Sera Monastery, the Jokhhang Temple, in their main square, his Winter Palace (the Potala), his Summer Palace (Norbulinka)--always there would be throngs of Tibetans who, though he had by this time escaped with his life to safety in India, still reverenced these venerated places. Unfortunately, the Han Chinese who had caused His Holiness to flee to safety were also in Tibet. Their army had invaded, seized any who defied them, tortured and killed more than one million civilians, raped their women--especially the nuns--and wreaked havoc wherever they went. Although I was thrilled with my experience as a tourist, I was devastated by their plight and promised myself that I would try to find out all I could and to become engrossed with all things Tibetan, especially Tenzin Gyatso, the 14th Dalai Lama, their beloved leader.

Visitors bought t-shirts that read "Free Tibet." I did as well, but we all knew it wouldn't be advisable to wear them until we were safe at home. Our accommodation was a No Star Guest House in a military compound. Its rating was definitely apropos. We had to climb three flights of stairs to arrive at a room that could only be described as pitiful--really no furniture other than two single beds, the sheets and pillow cases of which were soiled by former tenants. We slept with our clothes on! As well, we soon discovered that, once we were in the compound, we would be forbidden to leave unless accompanied by a Chinese National guide--and definitely not at night!

Anyway, back to my story. I considered Krys's proposal carefully, but my intense desire to meet the Dalai Lama, face to face, caused me to throw caution to the wind. My carefully composed letter of introduction to the Dalai Lama's secretary--his brother, Lobsang Samten--was already on its way to India. I'd told Krys to go ahead with the travel arrangements. I was hooked, once again. I was going to India. It would just be a formality but I thought I should at least make an announcement to my long-suffering family. Dead silence, until my daughter finally spoke. "Surely not, Mom! Remember all of the adversities you faced: the horrible heat in New Delhi, the political unrest in Kashmir, and near the hill stations of Gulmarg and Sonamarg... even Dharamsala. Don't you recall the awful hotels and restaurants, the filth and poverty...? Please Mom, say you're not going there again!"

My airline pilot son, John, chimed in with, "Not only would I not consider India a travel destination, I wouldn't even land there! Even worse, I heard that a bomb was found in an Air India Boeing 747 carrying 398 passengers and 18 crew members minutes before it was due to take off from New Delhi, for London and New York, just last week." Touché, I thought, I can always count on John. Had really hoped he would have missed that bit of news! Too late. A tirade of responses ensued with various family members giving opinions which ranged from "You're an idiot!" to "I really wish you wouldn't go."

My argument was that these things were always happening and were usually caught before departure. After all, the plane had been evacuated as soon as a steward found the bomb in a food trolley while he was making routine preflight checks of catering equipment. There were numerous other comments until my husband ended things with, "Do what you want. You will anyway!" He was never angry when he said this; just resigned. So, in two weeks I'd be off on my third trip to India and another of my exciting adventures.

I won't bore you with all of the annoying travel details of such things as long delays, annoying airport transfers, and forced layovers--so will begin with our arrival in New Delhi. The drive from the airport to the Imperial Hotel was, to put it mildly, a bit scary. Our maniacal driver must have been training for the Indy 500! The hotel? Let me see. In my star rating of hotels in Asia,

I will assign three stars to the Imperial. Why? Well, if you consider its construction, probably circa 1940, musty aroma, small beds with hard mattresses, and a view of a junkyard and construction shed, you may agree with my rating.

I have, thankfully, stayed in some of India's magnificent five star hotels. The Taj, in New Delhi, has a beautiful white marble lobby, with huge marble vases of wonderful flowers. It is one of the few Indian hotels I've stayed in, with five superb restaurants. My favorite was the French. Ooh la la! Jaipur's Rambagh Palace Hotel is equally luxurious in every way. Its Maharajah and Maharani suites have silk canopied beds, rich silk drapes, duvets, and covered divans. I felt like a Indian queen in mine!

So, on with the story. There's a great song I love: "One Scotch, One Bourbon, One Beer." So, according to my diary, I had decided to go with the Scotch and to desist in giving details of India's really rich, poor, and not so poor. My entry for August 7 was: "What can I say? It's India and, if you want things to be like home, you should stay at home."

The next day was all we had to confirm our travel details, arrange to have some of our luggage stored until our return from Dharamsala and to prepare for the following day's flight to the home of the Dalai Lama, near McLeod Ganj. This required a sortie out into the intense heat of the city and a cab ride to the travel agency. How hot was it? Well, I don't know the temperature of a blast furnace, but I believe the city's heat would have compared favorably! Memory tends to discard the bad parts of all of my former India trips, so I confess to having forgotten the heat, the smells, the poverty, cows in the streets, with their deposits everywhere.... No more complaining, Barb. This is India. Haven't you always declared that, in spite of all of the places you've visited, Kashmir, Tibet, and India are your favorites? If all goes well, in a few days you may find yourself in the presence of one of the world's most famous proponents of compassion and peace: His Holiness, the Dalai Lama.

Upon arrival to Dharamsala, Krys and I were transported to our hotel. The Bhagsu, according to Krys's guidebook, was the finest accommodation available in the Himalayan foothills. Mr. Hira Singh greeted us and offered to show us the choice of rooms. He recommended the VIP Suite. "You should know that the president of India always stays in the VIP when he is visiting the Dalai Lama at McLeod Ganj. I'm certain it will be just right for you. Very comfortable!"

Mr. Singh's manner was extremely gracious as he led us up the stairs. No elevator, but that's not uncommon in other than five star hotels in India. First impressions of the VIP were okay: acceptable furniture and decor, great pictures of local scenery and, of course, a wonderful painting of the Dalai Lama. However, following our first night we had to ratchet it down a bit. How could a room with rats running about in the ceiling and fleas in the bathroom qualify as VIP? Days later, from my diary: "The dogs are barking incessantly but the rats have settled down; the fleas seem to be trapped in the bathroom but Krys is wearing an eye mask in case some of the fleas still attack." We now had a new translation for VIP: Vermin Infested Premises!

The Bhagsu doesn't serve dinner, so Krys and I made our way down the hill to the business section of Dharamsala. The streets were narrow and our senses were bombarded with: hole in the wall shops, dirty (make that filthy) restaurants, guest houses, dirty people--Tibetan and Indian-- motor scooters and small cars battling their way past pedestrians, around tiny children, dogs, and puppies. Dodging muddy pot holes and messy cow flaps made driving even more of a challenge! One filthy guy with long stringy hair, bare feet, and a few tattered clothes, had

The Journey Itself

obviously dropped out of life. Many Dharamsalians are hippies--much like Kathmandu, but not as civilized.

We finally arrived at Krys's choice, again from her famous guide book. The Himalayan Restaurant was bad, really bad! I've never been in worse--and that's saying something because I've tested many of this ilk in third-world countries. A small boy, likely about eight years old, led us in past very soiled curtains to be seated at a dilapidated table with a bouquet of gold and maroon plastic flowers. Now about the menu. Okay, there wasn't a menu. Another small boy arrived to take our order. By this time, I had lost my appetite for anything, but Krys suggested the Tibetan Vegetable Momo, small pastries filled with vegetables, vegetable rice, chow mein, and curry so I went along with that. Mistake! Huge orders and a weird taste--probably the oil and garlic.

As Krys and I exited the restaurant, the dirty curtain screen into the kitchen was now pinned back. I took a quick look, and was sorry I did that. Our meal had come from this very kitchen. Even younger boys were standing on wooden boxes, stirring the contents of huge kettles, the lining of which was covered with thick scum of previously prepared delights. Yuk. Double yuk! Bet I'll pay for this later!

The following day we were determined to find out what we would have to do to contact the office of the Dalai Lama's secretary. Given that there had been no reply to my nine-page introduction letter requesting a private audience with His Holiness, there would undoubtedly be a certain protocol required. We went to the manager's office to attain the name of the appropriate contact person.

Hira greeted us enthusiastically. I had already sensed a certain eagerness on his part--directed specifically toward my friend Krys. Admittedly, Krys is extremely attractive: tall, slim, long black hair, great personality . . . in India, she could be taken for

Indian; in Mexico, Mexican. She turns heads whenever she enters a room. I do believe she had already turned the head of Mr. Hira Singh! "Good morning Miss Krystyna." His eyes flashed as he addressed her. "And you too, Madam Barbara." Always an afterthought, I mused. "How may I help you today?"

"We don't know if we mentioned it before," I began, "but we have come to Dharamsala on a very special mission. We are seeking a private audience with His Holiness, the Dalai Lama. I contacted his office a month or so ago approaching this very matter. You see, I was in Tibet in 1985. That visit to Lhasa really opened my eyes to the appalling atrocities which the Han Chinese have visited upon Tibetans! I took many wonderful photos of his people. A collection of the best are here in this book." I proffered said book so Hira could see. "It is my intention to present it to him. We received no reply to the letter; just came ahead hoping to verify that this would be possible now while we're here in Dharamsala. Perhaps you could help us with this."

Hira's expression registered concern. "I'm sorry to tell you, ladies, the Dalai Lama is away! I believe he has been visiting the Prime Minister of Australia and when he returns to India he will be conducting several discourses in Simla until he goes to New Delhi on August 15." Krys and I exchanged glances. Our train to Jodhpur and Jaisalmer, for our camel safari, departed Delhi on August 15. All this way for nothing. Okay, I thought, how will we salvage this goal? If nothing else, Hira might be able to get us an appointment to meet the Dalai Lama's secretary so he could deliver the promised book of photos to His Holiness.

At this point, Krys spoke up, "So Madam Barbara , what's the plan?"

"I may be able to help out a bit here, ladies. I have the business card for the Dalai Lama's liaison officer. Don't think there's much

The Journey Itself

use doing anything here, but he'd be the one to see when you get to New Delhi. As well, I'll write a letter of introduction for you to present to him. Now, about your flight. Perhaps we should change your departure for August 13. That will give you a day or so in Delhi to see if you can set up a meeting for the 15th." We were effusive with our thanks, and Hira said he was pleased to have helped. He seemed concerned that I had experienced a day or so of traveler's malaise, probably brought on by dining at the Himalayan Restaurant, and suggested that he would make it possible for us to dine at the Bhagsu from then on. We didn't know if he intended to join us, but he indicated that the arrangements would be made for dinner that night.

So the VIP suite received some of our attention that afternoon. Just a bit of a tidy-up, but it was presentable when a servant arrived at eight with a gift of incense and flowers. At 8:30, Hira appeared at our door with a beautiful bouquet. He had changed from his customary business suit and was wearing a stylish black suit with a great red tie. His announcement that he would be our server was given with a dramatic flair. "You must know, ladies, that I have been trained in some of India's finest hotels--even the Taj in Bombay." Hira directed this information specifically to Krys. This confirmed my suspicion about the real reason for all of the special attention.

Each course was served with finesse. The Tandoori chicken, nan (bread), and vegetables were served with a wine named Himalayan. We all enjoyed some pleasant conversation. Hira, his wife and children had been guests of the Dalai Lama. He had interesting things to tell us about that. We talked of Canada and other places we had visited in India. When the evening ended, Hira insisted that we must have dinner again the next evening, adding that he'd endeavor to find a more celebratory beverage. The menu would include Tandoori chicken again, with pacoras and papadans. If the weather permitted, he would love to take us on a guided tour of Sunset Point. I knew he wouldn't be disappointed if Madam Barbara declined, but I had no intention of going.

Krys had purchased a magnificent book entitled *Living Tibet*. It was filled with amazing pictures of places we wouldn't have time to visit. Among them were: The Library of Tibetan Arts and Archives, The School for Arts And Sciences, the Tibetan Institute of Performing Arts, and the Tibetan Children's Village School. When we showed our book to Hira, he insisted that we visit Namgyal temple and monastery. "You must see the true splendor of what the Dalai Lama and the Tibetan community have accomplished, in the four decades since they fled from their own country. It is much too far for you to walk. My friend, Jampal, will be your driver and guide for the day."

When Krys and I insisted that we would accept this generous offer only if we were allowed to pay something, Hira agreed that a tip would be quite acceptable. So with disappointments come bright spots of unexpected pleasure. We'd get to see some of the splendor that Tibet is renowned for worldwide. I will not take the time that would be required to give a detailed account, so will just mention the immense Kalachakra mandala that fills the entire west wall of the Namgyal temple, and the altar, which is decorated with an amazing fresco, featuring Shakyamuni Buddha at the center. Picture, if you will, towering walls, the expanses of which are decorated with Buddhist iconography, resplendent in gold, scarlet, and black. We were overwhelmed! For me, it brought back the feelings of wonder that I had experienced at the Potala Palace and the Sera Monastery in Lhasa.

By now, I hope you will see the dramatic difference between the negativity with which I began this narrative and the contrasting details that delineate India's beauty. I stand by the fact that I truly do love India, Tibet, and Kashmir. In the entire world, they

The Journey Itself

were my favorite trips! Then too, I must confess to having an inexplicable feeling whenever I find myself in the foothills of the Himalayas. No particular reason. It just happens. So, when Krys and I set out on our first walkabout from the Bhagsu Hotel, the magic began.

We were surrounded by scenery which is representative of Tibet. Our route followed a mountainous incline to the upper level of McLeod Ganj. Its beautiful trees and wildflowers, and rocky hillsides studded with Himalayan oak, urged us on until we could see in the valley, 4000 feet below, the deep hunter-green of evergreens and soft yellow-green of deciduous trees. To the north lay the 15,000-foot Dhauladhar Range, with its snowy crags and peaks. I don't know about Krys, but I was in heaven--again.

Proof of my delight can be found in a book of my favorite poems and souvenirs that I have saved from my trips. On page 74, the caption, beside some tiny wildflowers, reads: "August 11, 1992. Ah the fragility of life! " I picked these not far from the Dalai Lama's private residence, near the Thekchen Choeleng Cathedral, near Mcleod Ganj. Their survival depended on the small plastic pouch that held them until my return to Canada. As I placed them on the page, and attempted to cover them with tape, they leapt up to cling to their protector. For, you see, they had lost the moisture of life and were in danger of crumbling and being swept away by the slightest breath."

August 13, the day of our flight from Kangra airport to New Delhi, began well. Hira had arranged for an early breakfast in our room so we could be driven to the airport for an early morning departure. The weather? Promising, though the monsoon season was about to begin. The cab driver had been advised to wait until our flight left, but assured us there would be no problem. His words: "Your flight is sure to go!" Ah yes, Barbara, remember your pony man from the ill-fated trek always said the same thing…"No problem, Madam. No problem."

About ten minutes after he left, I was in the washroom when I heard Krys announce, "It's canceled! They have reconfirmed us for tomorrow, but that won't do. It could be canceled again, and that would mean we'd get into Delhi the very day the Dalai Lama is expected to arrive from Simla."

At this point I said, "If we didn't have bad luck we wouldn't have any luck at all, Krys. Now it's your turn to come up with Plan B."

"Okay, Madam Barbara, we'll just go back to the Bhagsu and get Hira's advice. Can't sleep in the airport, can we!" Hira suggested that we stay at the hotel and try again the next day. By now, I think we both knew what he wanted. Despite the fact that he was married with children, there were any number of indications that, given a day or so more, he might be able to convince Miss Krystyna to spend time with him--alone. When we insisted that we must leave the next day, Hira seemed disappointed, but said he knew a taxi driver who could be hired for the thirteen-hour drive to Delhi. We were to depart at 3:00 a.m. and hopefully arrive by around 4:00 p.m. that same day. Please notice that I have said "hopefully."

The next morning we bid our friendly hotel manager goodbye, with our assurance that he could not have been more helpful, adding that it was greatly appreciated. We hadn't asked him for his mailing address, but it was given anyway. Wonder why? Krys and I both agreed that, in most cases, Indian people have generous, warm personalities. My prior experiences--our pony trek in the Himalayas and home stay experience with Bombay millionaires--were further proof of this. The cab arrived, and so our perilous journey began. In the event that you are thinking, "How perilous could it be? Except for the time constraints, you would be able to just sit back and relax," allow me to say: You may have heard of, or even experienced, a white-knuckle trip. However, I wager it was not on India's mountain roads or in the frantic traffic of the Punjab on "Brothers' and Sisters" Day!

We tried to console ourselves with the fact that our driver's front seat passenger was the owner of said taxi. This might affect his driving performance when confronted with fallen boulders ahead, winding roads with no possible way to pass, and iffy braking of his vehicle. If the constant, overly loud Indian music throughout the entire trip was intended to ease our minds, it only heightened our distress. All those hours and neither of us said a word--a few gasps, but no words!

The Punjab, in Sikhdom, presented different hazards. Undoubtedly the Sikh holiday would have accounted for a steady stream of buses loaded with hundreds on their way to local festivals. I must remind you that Indian buses are nothing like our own--more like a vehicle with cobbled-up sheets of tin, decorated with gaudy colors and pictures of religious icons. Many revelers stood up top; others were jammed into the backs of pick-up trucks. We witnessed the aftermath of at least twelve accidents. A truck and a bus were totally smashed up...the truck getting the worst of it. An old van, with Indian dancers painted on the sides, had been further decorated with great smears of blood. No vehicle had remained at the scene, but there was one dead horse whose life had suddenly come to an inauspicious end.

As the trip progressed, we learned that the driver's name was Surinda; his boss was Mr. Sakeem. When Surinda told us that we were travelling the Grand Trunk Road #1, Krys whispered that we should have T-shirts made that said, "I survived the Grand Trunk ride from Dharamsala to Delhi --that's providing we actually do get there!" We didn't dare to speak it aloud, but I can imagine we both were thinking the same thing. In the event of an accident, the possibility of our survival would be slim. No police, no ambulance, no hospital…and not likely any English spoken!

At one of our rest stops, we were able to gain an overview of the reckless traffic: cars passed on the right, where it seemed impossible to pass; there were several near misses; a dead mule, with its cart overturned, hindered the progress of a few; the never ending horn-blowing just went on and on! Krys said her mother would kill her if she knew where we were. Then it was on our way again with crossed fingers and some prayers to Allah, Buddha, Lord Krishna, our God . . . whoever would listen and come to our aid!

Many hours and several rest stops later, we arrived at the Imperial Hotel. Surprisingly, the cost was much less than we had expected, and Madam Barbara gave Surinda a huge tip. Words could not express how thankful we were to have survived the Grand Trunk ride! As we entered the lobby we heaved a sigh of relief and perhaps to demonstrate her relief, Krys quipped, "Hi, honey. I'm home."

Although we enjoyed a pleasant breakfast at the Imperial Hotel, there was little time to consider other than our rather desperate attempt to discover someone who might be able to make our dream come true. Fortunately, Krys had a good friend in New Delhi. Sashi Mohran's husband was a lieutenant general with the Indian Army. He had agreed to take us to Tibet House, and we were off to try our luck there. From the air-conditioned hotel into 50 degrees Celsius (120 degrees F) was really hard to take, but we were on a mission! The contact at Tibet House was very agreeable, looked at my book of Tibetan photos, listened to our story, and advised us to go to the Dalai Lama's office. So it was back out into the insufferable heat and on to try our luck again. How hot was it? Well, we had just showered, and shampooed and dried our hair, and within minutes of exiting the air-conditioned hotel, our hair was dripping wet and our clothes were clinging to our bodies.

We were fortunate to have Sashi's husband as our private chauffeur, or it would have meant getting a cab, asking the driver to wait, and paying for the service. Once again we were greeted by a very amiable gentleman. The same procedure: presentation of my gift of photos for His Holiness and recounting of our request to be granted a private audience. Surely the Dalai Lama's private secretary would have the authority to do just that! From the look on Dorje's face, I realized we weren't going to receive good news. "Very sorry, so very sorry! Tomorrow is the biggest holiday of the year, in India. It will be a celebration of Independence Day. All stores will be closed and the streets will be awash with crowds of people. What's more, the Dalai Lama's flight is not expected until about 3:00 p.m. and, with all of the traffic . . . ."

Krys and I must have looked heavy-hearted...and we certainly were that. Our overnight train to Jaisalmer, for our camel safari, would depart Delhi station at 6:30 p.m. Even if we were granted an audience, it would have to occur by 4:30 p.m. We'd still have to pick up our packed bags from our own hotel and get to the train station. In view of the improbability of a happy outcome, which would mean crisscrossing the maze of city streets, I suggested that it might be best for me to leave the book of photos with Dorje. Apparently, this triggered his sympathy, for he said, "It seems such a pity that you have come all this way, from Canada, to see the Dalai Lama only to be disappointed! Keep the pictures with you and I will see what I can do. I'll call you at the Imperial Hotel if I have any success." We were then driven to the Delhi Gymkana Club to meet Sashi for lunch. The club is very private—accessible only to military men and their families.

Thank God it was air conditioned, as the extreme heat was making me feel quite ill. Cold coffee with ice cream and sandwiches brightened me up a bit, but I declined the deep fried chicken (tikka) ordered for Krys. Back at our hotel, Krys went for a swim and I lay down, totally exhausted. I slept until our phone rang at 3:00 p.m. It was Dorje! I was so excited I almost dropped the phone. "Yes, you have your private audience at 4:45 p.m. but you must be at the Oshaka Hotel by 4:30 p.m." I replied that I thought he was wonderful and that I could never adequately express my delight. I thanked him from the bottom of my heart and added my utmost gratitude.

If you had been at the Ashoka Hotel, on the afternoon of August 15, you would have found two very nervous Canadians bearing cameras, gifts, and the traditional white silk khatas (ceremonial scarves), to present to Tenzin Gyatso, the Fourteenth Dalai Lama of Tibet. Although our meeting was scheduled for 4:45 p.m., we had arrived early and sat impatiently in the lobby. At 4:45 we had still not been summoned and we grew apprehensive. Was the Dalai Lama's flight delayed? Had there been a miscommunication? Had we come all this way, and crossed so many hurdles, only to be met with yet another disappointment? Krys went to reception to inquire and to show the liaison officer's business card, which we had been given when we were in Dharamsala. It worked. Moments later, we were escorted to a small waiting room on the third floor. The Dalai Lama had been late arriving, and several other audiences were backed up, but now provision had been made for us. We were next.

Our friend, Dorje, came to offer instruction in the Tibetan way of presenting the ceremonial khatas. However, in less than a minute, another gentleman arrived and said that we must come quickly. His Holiness was waiting for us. Our cameras and bags were inspected and we were ushered into a beautifully decorated reception room. Bouquets of red roses were set out on

The Journey Itself

white marble tables; a huge elephant, painted black, red and gold, was positioned in a corner near the brocaded divan where the Dalai Lama was sitting. However, my admiration of the decor paled when the Dalai Lama rose and walked toward me. He was wearing the traditional maroon over saffron monk's robes, and his olive-tinted glasses, but it was his smile, his warmth... his aura that lit up the room.

I put the binder of photos on a table and began the presentation of the khata that I had brought for him. Gone were any of Dorje's instructions! I just bowed; uttered the traditional "Namaste" and said, "Your Holiness, this is such a great joy." Once again, his amazing smile as he placed the silk scarf around my neck and asked me to be seated in a chair next to him. I had read that the Dalai Lama always endeavors to engage his visitors in a warm personal exchange, and here I was experiencing that very thing.

I should tell you that the photos I was about to present were all taken during my 1985 trip to Tibet. Some were at the Sera Monastery; some in his winter palace, the Potala; others at the Norbulingka, or summer palace. My main focus had been on his beautiful people--Tibetans who had not fled their country with the Chinese invasion of 1950. He turned each page and made numerous comments. At the one of me in an Indian sari, he chuckled and said, "Indian!" Another was of our Tibetan guide. At this point he spoke to his aides asking, "How would he learn English?" The photo I had taken on the road to Lhasa was of Tibetan peasants and a small boy wearing a military hat. Again his wonderful giggle as he pointed to the child. We had not been allowed to photograph any of the altars at the Potala Palace, but there had been a beautiful little one in an alcove and I was unable to resist. I pointed to it now and said, "Potala Palace."

His comment was, "No! No! Not Potala!" Now you must realize that the Potala was Tenzin Gyatso's home from the time he was a very small boy. He ascended the throne at age six and was confirmed at age 15, I believe. So he would have spent every winter there until his escape in 1959. He would surely know every inch of that palace. In my embarrassment, I hastily added, "I must be mistaken, sir." Now, I ask you, why would I have addressed a humble man, who wants to be known as a simple Buddhist monk, as sir? When Krys asked for permission to take a picture of me with him, one of his attendees announced that the Dalai Lama loves to have his picture taken. This was accomplished, and then it was Krys's turn.

She moved to a chair near him and proffered a very large Toblerone chocolate bar that she had purchased at the airport in London, England. They spoke briefly. Krys had followed the Dalai Lama's life since she was ten years old. She had also been in the crowd that lined his exit from our parliament buildings during one of his visits to Ottawa in the nineties. As their conversation ended, she asked if we might both pose for another photo with him. We sat on either side of this dynamic public figure; he closed his right hand around my left and his left around Krys's right. You could feel the amazing energy flowing from him to us. What a marvelous experience that was! At this point he asked for two copies of one of his books to be brought to him, signed each book, then pointed out the Tibetan words above his signature, saying, "That's a prayer."

It was over then. Two highly elated Canadians had enjoyed a private audience with Tenzin Gyatso, Fourteenth Dalai Lama of Tibet. All we had to do now was get a taxi back to our hotel; pick up our bags, and arrive at the station in time for the 6:00 p.m. train to Jaisalmer, where we would begin our next adventure, in Rajasthan. I must remind you that it was Independence Day in India and the traffic was in chaos! Did we make it? That's another story, which will appear in the account of the Camel Safari in Rajasthan.

Camel Safari in Rajasthan

Immediately following our exciting audience with the Dalai Lama, our next challenge was to head back to our hotel, pick up our luggage, which we had checked in the lobby, hire a taxi, and make haste to the train station. Our train tickets said 6:45 p.m. departure and it was already 5:45 p.m. You may be thinking that we should be able to make it in an hour, but I must inform you that we were in New Delhi, it was Independence Day in India, and all of the streets were choked with traffic.

All was total confusion. Horns were blaring, and most of the traffic rules thrown to the wind. Were Krys and I concerned? I must confess that we were quite giddy, complacent, even smug, with what we had just accomplished. We both agreed that we did not care at all about catching the train. We had met His Holiness-- just the two of us with the Dalai Lama!

Finally, at the station, we handed our bags to porters who proceeded to the appropriate car. My guy had bags over each shoulder, my video camera on his head, and was walking much too fast for me to keep up. I could hear Krys shouting, "Don't lose sight of him, or all your stuff will be gone!" Fortunately that didn't happen and we were ushered into a train compartment for four people. We complimented ourselves on having the whole space to ourselves and began to unpack a few things. I took a picture of Krys on a top bunk having a drink from her bottle of rum. And she did the same of me on a bottom bunk across from her. With a drink? Of course, it seemed appropriate for me to toast the situation with my favorite drink of Scotch!

The train pulled out of the station with two very happy travelers. We had brought some snacks, so we enjoyed these and the ride until the next stop. Little did we know that the honeymoon was almost over. A porter arrived with other people for our compartment. Two more would have been okay but the group of Indian people included a mother, wearing a purple sari, with a ten-month- old baby; a lady in an orange sari and green scarf, with a two-year-old boy; plus a gentleman dressed in beige slacks and shirt. They all seemed quite clean and the compartment was air- conditioned but, despite the fan, that was a lot of bodies in one small space on a hot day in India! The lady with the two-year-old sat next to me on my bottom bunk. I emphasize "my", as I had no intention of climbing up to the top. She kept pointing up and I kept shaking my head in the negative. So it was finalized. She and child went up. The lady with the baby stayed on the other lower bunk, and Krys was on the upper. The gentleman? He chose to sleep on the floor between the bunks. So I could look forward to climbing over him when I went to the bathroom during the night. I use the word bathroom loosely, as it was a hole in the floor at the end of the car. One stood on tiptoe as most of the fluid on the floor could not possibly be water but urine which had somehow missed the hole!

One might wonder about the chances of getting any sleep in this situation. However, I did manage to catch some shut-eye, albeit complete with weird dreams of teaching a grade eight class which had never heard of nouns or adjectives! By morning, I was aware of a strange smell-- hopefully just of sweating bodies. It clung to me and Krys even after we had departed the train.

The Journey Itself

Mr. Jethram Choudhary from Rajasthan Tours sought us out and announced that he would be our driver. Once we were loaded into his small blue diesel car we were off to Jodhpur and thence to Jaisalmer, one of the most important cities on the ancient Silk Road. He struck up a conversation right away--one which, we were to learn, would be more than we would have wished for during our six-hour trip! When he learned that we were from Canada, of course he had a friend in Canada and he too would like to go to Canada. He hoped to get a job there. It would be quite wonderful if he could only get this opportunity. My thoughts went to, Touché. Where have I heard this before? It is one of the many cons. Just like "Pen for school?" with no school within a hundred-mile radius, and the Kashmiri "No need to buy. Only look!"

Our silence did not deter Jethram. He was on a roll and we were his captive audience. "Mama," he said, "I making every kind of work for you, in Canada." Mama; so already I'm his mother--never an endearing feature for one having a conversation with me. It reminded me of always being addressed as Madam Barbara while Krys got Miss Krystyna. Admittedly my age was obvious. I was, after all, sixty-plus; I just didn't like to acknowledge it.

I ventured that I lived on a farm, and asked what experience he would have for working on a farm. I should have expected his answer: "I making every kind of work for you: planting, look after animals--even work in house cooking and cleaning...." I let Krys answer his questions about how much money he would make and how much it would cost to live in Canada, as well as how cold Canada's winters were. When he wanted to know, "How far Canada? How long to get there? How much costing?" We threw out some large numbers and he fell silent for a short time.

However, he began once more with great enthusiasm. He would give me his address and then I could send him the money to come. "Like do all kinds of work! Farm work, yes! Drive car! Making food! Everything!" Poor sweet misguided man. If only he knew how unlikely this would ever be--not just with me, but with anyone. Krys and I changed the subject and began asking questions about India. Jethram seemed to understand, and was very polite about adding to our knowledge of his country. By this time I believe he was just hoping for a good tip. Finally, our conversation slowed to an occasional question Krys or I had for our friendly cab driver, and we were able to enjoy the scenery.

It was my first long drive through Rajasthan and I marveled at the desert scenery. Lots of sand, of course, with many parts of the road drifted with sand--just like our winter snow drifts. There's no melting here--just people like us, perspiring in the intense heat! Along the roads we passed hundreds of goats, sheep, and cows being herded along by one or two herdsmen. The sheep were tall black ones with curly ears, though a few were white. The goats were various breeds and, of course, there were camels. Supposedly, it was monsoon time, but we saw no rain at all. A few fields were green with millet; some had corn; and others were dotted with what I believed to be some kind of cactus. It's a wonder the animals can survive.

Jethram was a very good driver, though he had nothing to contend with compared to our trip from Dharamsala to Delhi! Every once in a while we were slowed down by roads under construction. The labor force here was Rajasthani women in the most gorgeous silk apparel. Yes, doing heavy arduous work with picks and shovels and carrying baskets of rocks on their heads! All of this in a 100 degrees F or more! We passed right through Jodhpur, as Krys would be starting her camel safari from Jaisalmer. We had made very good time--Jodhpur to Jaisalmer in five and a half hours instead of six hours, with only one stop at a filthy restaurant, which really didn't qualify as a restaurant. Jethram put two chairs outside for us and added another chair for our table. I can't believe I ate or drank anything in such a disgusting place, but you get so desperately thirsty, driving in the desert!

We went on then to our hotel, where I was to get the shock of my life. My home for the next six days, formerly a stable for camels, lay before us. Yes, the Narayan Niwas Palace Hotel was supposed to be the best in Jaisalmer. Actually it was a paint-worn desert hotel like one might see in Mexico. Our room had two twin beds pushed together in a very small space. A Rajput border design, in ugly yellow, decorated walls that had once been white. There was no place to put our clothes--just a couple of hooks in a small alcove. However, you might look at it this way. It was a real bargain pricewise, at $13.92 US per day.

I believe I have omitted the best and the worst of our little desert hideaway! The best was the fan. It did cool us just a little bit, as well as helping to move the flies about. The worst? With no windows or screens, millions of flies loved our No-Star room as well! As I mention No-Star accommodations, I am reminded of a similar experience in a guest house in Lhasa, Tibet. The Narayan Niwas Palace Hotel was much worse. Mind you, unlike the Tibet experience of turning down the bed to discover the sheet covered with pubic hairs, at least this desert hotel had clean bedding. The help sprayed our room and made a brave attempt to control the flies, but to no avail. Krys and I gave in, commenting that we had no hope of being Lord of the Flies!

In the afternoon Krys and I walked down to town. I'd say it was probably 105 F. Krys said my face was scarlet, and I was having difficulty keeping up to her pace. Our mission was to go to the bank and our tour Company, Rajasthani Tours. Cows, dogs, sheep, goats, and a few camels were everywhere in the streets. Oh! Did I forget the flies? The smell of animal dung assaulted our nostrils and remained with us. Some enterprising kids asked for pens or rupees; musicians wanted to play for us; shopkeepers tried to call us in. Small children crouched over the gutters to defecate, and hordes of flies descended to feast on the new source of food.

Okay, I'll spare you. No more gross details. We had arrived at the tour office and Krys confirmed all necessary details. She'd go out on the camels for two or three days and I'd stay by myself in Fly City. If I wanted, some of the guys would take me out for dinner in the desert. That sounded a bit risky for me, but I'm usually game for anything, and my experiences in India had previously been that tourists were respected. I'd let them know.

My physical condition registered really poor. The heat, the food, and some other problems would likely prevent dinner in the desert. That night was filled with really foolish dreams of my trying to take pictures of friends I hadn't seen in years, but by morning I was able to bid Krys goodbye and give a possible "yes" to my desert dates. A rest, and some good old Italian spaghetti, allowed me to tell Narpat Singh that I was up for our desert adventure. He and the other two guys would pick me up in their Jeep at 5:30. The sandy route was quite rough and we did get stuck once, but my dates got it back on the path. I was actually looking forward to the night. At least it would be cooler. One of the guys said it had been 56 C in June the previous year, and many people had died. Those without much shelter, and no electricity or running water, would literally be scorched in the burning heat.

Suddenly, as we left the main road, Narpat said, "There's your friend's tent. She must be sleeping. See over by those bushes." Sure enough, there was Miss Krystyna seated on a Rajasthani carpet--magic, of course! She was reading one of her novels.

The Journey Itself

Krys has to be he most adaptable person I know--never a problem, given any situation. As I write this I must include her confession to me later on. The first night she had experienced such a blinding headache that she was unable to stand. The terrific heat and lack of water were causing her to have second thoughts about going out again the next day. Fred, her camel, the two-year-old, and another male, had been released for the evening.

The guide made me most welcome and served Indian tea--milk, spices, and sugar cooked with the tea. At least I certainly hope so, as water and milk were not safe to drink unless they were boiled. Then it was time for a real drink. I said I would share a beer with the boys, but when Krys got out the vodka and they brought real squeezed lemon juice, I did change my mind. It was superb and we each enjoyed two of these.

The camel men brought Fred over, put on the saddle, and permitted me to have a short ride around the camp. A Raj led me, so I wasn't afraid Fred would take off. So now I had experienced pony rides, elephant rides, and camel rides. How lucky is that?

Narpat said the desert was right next to Pakistan and that we might like to go there some time. Our suggestion that it might be dangerous was denied. However, we thanked him but answered in the negative. Both Kashmir and Pakistan were fighting again since I'd been there some years before.

I will be unable to convey the beauty of that night, but I'll try. There was a soft breeze, as there had been all day; the browns and mauves of sand were exquisite, and there was just enough greenery of shrubs and cactus for contrast. Other Indian families were camped here, some distance from our camp. By comparison, Miss Krystyna's tent was small, but it was multi colored and made of cotton. I assumed the cotton made it cooler.

The sunset was beautiful, but I was not able to capture it on film. There was lightning, in the distance but no threat of a storm and the sky above us was filled with thousands of blinking stars. As the night darkened, candles on decorated standards were lit and dinner was served. We were seated on a beautiful Rajasthani magic carpet and a flute player had been employed to entertain us. A most wonderful dinner was served: a soup made of tomato and chicken with herbs, but not too spicy; next a huge plate of mashed potatoes with rice, chicken, mutton, dal, and a curry that I didn't try. I'd had a bad experience when I had given in to a truly spicy meal, in Chengdu, China and paid a serious price for my experiment. Madam Barbara cannot eat spicy food! Next we were served my favorite, crème caramel with a wonderful coffee.

Back to the flute player. The instrument seemed to have two flutes combined and he played sad love songs of desert Maharajahs and various other Rajasthani legends. We clapped each time and Krys gave him 50 ra. When I learned the recipe for moola, I was glad we didn't try that. "In a bowl, add grated moola or radish, bengal gram paste, mustard paste, coconut paste, coconut milk, green chili, sugar, coriander paste, oil, salt to taste, mix well and keep aside. Place a banana leaf in sunlight for 30 minutes to soften it a bit so that it doesn't crack on folding."

At 9:00 p.m. I suggested that we should get back to my hotel--and I use the term hotel loosely. Narpat's wife would be waiting for dinner until he arrived. I was delivered back to my hotel and sat outside listening to the music there for a while. At midnight I decided I really should try to sleep, though I was still reveling in the wonderful experience of "our dinner in the desert."

To be in Jaisalmer is to have been transported back in time to medieval Rajasthan--the land of the Tales of Arabian Nights, and

The Journey Itself

the Camel Train Route of the famous Silk Road. In the evening, the golden city is aglow as the sun is reflected on the sandstone ramparts of some of those beautiful old buildings. Centuries ago, Jaisalmer was one of the most strategic positions on the camel train routes. The merchants and townspeople built magnificent houses and mansions, all exquisitely carved from wood and from golden yellow sandstone. These Havelis are located elsewhere in Rajasthan but nowhere else as exotic as these. With the rise of the shipping trade and the popularity of the port of Bombay, Jaisalmer declined. Despite this, with the 1965-71 Indo -Pakistani wars, Jaisalmer once again became a strategic point of import. The Rajasthan Canal, to the north, prompted a restoration to life in the desert. Paved roads and railways now link it to the rest of Rajasthan. Even electricity has finally reached this remote part of India. When I wrote this in 1992, I could never have imagined that such a serious war would occur involving Pakistan, Afghanistan, Kashmir, and India. The whole world seems to have gone crazy, now in 2013!

Back to the camel safari. I enjoyed a good night's sleep and a delightful breakfast--the first real breakfast since I left home: orange juice, good porridge, scrambled eggs, and coffee. Then I went back to my favorite spot to be seated in a high-backed wicker chair, in front of a huge fan. The breeze was great and the flies deterred from bothering me. By noon, though, I was assured of another scorcher of a day. I planned some writing, reading, and shopping before another flight to the desert for dinner. Narpat said he'd pick me up at 6:00 p.m., but I expected he would be late as usual. His excuse for being half an hour late was that he had to take one of his clients to the hospital. As I thought about the hospital, I hoped that would never be my fate. If you were just a bit sick when you went in, the flies would make sure you'd be worse in a few days!

Narpat's wife had waited for him the night before and was suspicious that he had been drinking. My dates had spent more time with their outfits, probably to impress Miss Krystyna and Madam Barbara. Narpat was wearing a smart turquoise, pink, and blue-striped shirt; Rajpat wore a brown jacket, despite the heat, and had paid special attention to his curled Rajasthani mustache. Gianje´ and Narpat arrived with a much nicer Jeep, with Raj and Narpat sitting in the back and I in the front with the Gianjé, who was our driver. I was wearing the new Indian outfit I had purchased: loose-fitting burgundy cotton pants; and striped lilac, maroon, and green top--also cotton and loose-fitting. My silver and cornelian jewelery was a great match with the outfit.

So Madam Barbara and her "desert dates" were off for another lovely evening. The trip out was quite picturesque, with cows, sheep, goats, sweet little children, old men with white beards... and everywhere, brightly colored Rajasthani turbans and the vibrant hues of women's attire. The whole scene was certainly one out of the past--at least one hundred years ago. We drove in a different direction over very rough roads, then headed out through the sand dunes and riverbed.

Gianjé twisted and turned, with very abrupt wheel turning and maneuvering to get through the drifts of sand. I assured myself we would not upset, but hung on to the bar in front of me just in case. Raja hung on with one hand, but kept watch outside the Jeep on his side to alert the driver of anything untoward. Soon we arrived at the campsite where Miss Krystyna and Suma were walking up on a high ridge of sand. Krys reported a good day. They had gone about seven miles with stops at a village, two schools, and a fort. However, the intense heat had caused her to have such a terrific headache that she wished she was back in Jaisalmer. Her head pounded and when she tried to stand, she was very dizzy. So it would seem that the lady who was impervious to anything had met her match with Rajathan's desert heat!

Shortly after our arrival the carpet was spread out again and Suma asked if we would like some tea or coffee. I chose coffee with milk--very daring on my part, unless the milk was boiled too. Shortly, we were given another choice: lemonade, Limka, vodka, or rum and Pepsi. I thought Muslims were forbidden to drink liquor, but apparently, under certain conditions, it was okay! We toasted again to another pleasant evening and our desert dinner with good friends. The menu was similar to the previous night: a wonderful soup, mutton stew with mushrooms and vegetables, some potatoes, and best of all, a superb dessert--a caramel-glazed cake with coffee and Indian rum. As soon as dinner was over, they put out the lights so we could enjoy the canopy of the desert night, full of thousands and thousands of glittering stars. I was reminded of that poem by Wordsworth:

> And the night shall be filled with music,
> And the cares, that infest the day,
> Shall fold their tents, like the Arabs
> And as silently steal away.
>
> William Wordsworth

Our male companions spoke of politics and forthcoming business commitments, so I suggested that it might be time for me to get back to my hotel. They seemed relieved, as their women weren't happy if they were late, particularly if they smelled of alcohol. Miss Krystyna would return by noon the next day and had asked me to fill the bathtub to the top with cold water! That was my plan for that very evening. However, I did sit outside watching the dancers and listening to the music. I did not stay long, as I soon discovered that "Raja Rock" was not my cup of tea! The dancer was dressed in a cinnamon and bittersweet dress and veil. She wore gold bracelets from elbow to shoulder on both arms. Long, dangling bells were attached to her dress and tinkled as she swirled and swirled. I was impressed by her dancing and lingered for one more cold drink. When I noticed that it was midnight, I retired to my "suite" in the former camel stable, turned the fan on, and flopped on the bed. The next day I planned to go on a walkabout, taking video and immersing myself in this ancient culture.

August 19, 9:40 a.m. and I was sitting in my regular spot: the lovely lobby bar. I must say that it was very kind of me to have named it thus. The old wicker chairs were all "ratty." Small bits of straw decorated the dirt floor, and already millions of flies had found me. The power had been off for an hour that morning, so no fans running for even that short a time had made my room intolerable. At least there was a faint breeze outside. My breakfast was a contest between me and the flies. I had to hold my napkin over my glass of orange juice, whip it off, and take a quick sip before I recovered the glass. I'm proud to say that hardly any flies beat me to the draw! Actually the breakfast was quite good: oatmeal porridge and a whole pot of tea. Dehydration in this heat causes the bowels to dry up so that only a few hard feces make their way down for a very painful exit. Please excuse the very graphic description, but it is one of the serious problems of travelling in India. Either that or the unbelievably relentless diarrhea I have had frequently in these hot countries, particularly when I have taken malaria pills or eaten spicy food.

The following day I entertained myself by going about the streets, taking video of the ancient buildings, the shops, and animals wandering at their leisure. There were shops, markets, and little restaurants galore, but I decided a relatively "clean" place to eat would be at my hotel. How I wished our departure would be that very night, but that was not in the cards. True, this had been an unusual adventure, particularly the flights to the desert for dinner, but all in all not one the average tourist would ever consider. I always gave in to Krys, and she loved this sort of thing. However, I believe her terrible headaches and sunstroke symptoms had intimidated even my audacious friend this time.

I did stop for a beer, which was cold when served but soon became very warm. In Rajasthan, beer is rather expensive--48 ra or $1.65 US, but then the bottle was quite large. At a handicraft store, I bought seven pillow shams adorned with camels, and two tablecloths that had little mirrors on them. These are quite typical of Jaisalmer, and would make good gifts for those who were wise enough to stay in Canada. The tablecloths cost 1900 ra or $68 US each. I did go to the famous 12th-century Jaisalmer Fort, but did not linger further, and took a rickshaw back to the hotel.

Miss Krystyna was back and insisted that we go for Chinese food. Again with the Chinese food. Krys must have been in India too long, as she seemed to have adopted Indian tastes. Actually, it was very good: chow mein with chicken and almonds, and beer. Another beer? You'll be thinking I'm a lush. But remember, I did have to keep hydrated! Okay, I know beer dehydrates the drinker, but it feels good going down! Krys wanted some pillow shams and a tablecloth too, so we did that and, once again, had a rickshaw ride back to the hotel. Suma arrived at 4:00 p.m. and I paid for my dinners. Only $15 for two great adventures in the Thar Desert. What a bargain!

I won't gross you out again with the details of my condition for the following two days. All you need to know is that it was a recurrence of an all-too-familiar dysentery I have experienced so many times in India. A doctor saw me and threatened me with a visit to the hospital. That was enough to cure me almost immediately!

With all bills settled we headed to the train station on August 20. We were off to Jodhpur. Narpat was late as usual, so we called a taxi. Read Jeep. Then he showed up and took us and our bags, plus bed rolls, and helped us find our compartment on the train. Krys was a bit abrupt with him, as he had no written bill. He said it was to be a verbal agreement and transaction. She gave in and we settled into a rather nice compartment with two young people from Wales. In spite of the fact that ours was to be a first-class compartment, we had no air conditioning--only fans. However, it was bearable and after a while we had an interesting conversation with our new friends. They knew a young traveller who had been asked to share a hotel room with an Indian fellow. The next morning, when he awoke, he thought he had been drugged. All his stuff was gone: money, passport, even the gold chain from around his neck. So, you see thievery exists everywhere.

We were pleasantly surprised when we reached our hotel in Jodhpur. It was much more befitting Miss Krystyna and Madam Barbara; it even had air conditioning in the bed sitting room. The ceilings were about twelve feet high and the furniture and antiques quite beautiful. The beds had ornately carved headboards. As well, there were a writing desk and a mirrored glass cabinet with a huge mirror. We wondered about the fireplace. God knows when it would be needed. It really did seem out of place in this hot country. The love seat and armchairs were covered with a soft green fabric decorated with pink roses. The drapes at the entrance, and those on the huge windows, matched these. Beyond this room was a dressing room with a large armoire for our clothes and a lovely dressing table. Through two more doors we found a spacious bathroom with both tub and shower, and wonderful fans. The bed sitting room was the only room with air conditioning. Antiques and and huge paintings of Maharajahs and Maharanis gave proof to the fact that this had once been the Maharajah's home.

The Journey Itself

I feel compelled to tell you a little of the history. Many years ago, Jodhpur and other states of the Rathore kingdom were known as "Rumi" (The Land of Death). If by some chance, Jaisalmer was not included in this grouping, I hereby declare that it was also the epitome of killer heat and millions of flies. One evening when we were still staying at the former Maharajah's home, they had a magnificent buffet dinner. The waiters were all in typical Rajasthani garb, and the busboys in grey uniforms with black tams. The tables were adorned with gorgeous flowers and delightful candles that were lit from below. At either end rose the beautiful Rajasthani palace walls: red sandstone with intricate filigree.

At one end of the grand hall, the hot buffet was displayed. The food was set up in copper cooking vessels, as the Rajasthani believe that good vibrations come from food cooked in such a way. I know we experienced said vibrations throughout the entire evening. The copper ware was set over recessed pits, which were filled with live coals from time to time. On either side of the hot buffet table were large winged horses of sandstone, bearing the Maharajah's eagle crest, and in the corners, where the walls joined the balconies, were beautiful climbing pink flowers which reminded me of bougainvillea. The musicians, in red Raj turbans, played throughout. It was not the whining music that is so common in India, but a lot of drums and flutes. A small boy, dressed in a white royal costume and red turban, performed many special dances.

We were seated with a large group of Italians, so our conversation was definitely limited. However all in all it was a pleasant evening. The menu consisted of white rice, dal, a salty yogurt with something spicy in it, millet cooked with tomatoes, a potato dish, and a meat dish--probably lamb. I was still being careful, as I had no wish to repeat my experiences in Dharamsala or Jaisalmer. Hence the daily doses of Bactrim, anti-diarrhea medicine, and electrolytes…the latter of which tasted like the poison named Citromag which I have been forced to take prior to colonoscopies. Oh, I have forgotten the dessert, always my favorite part of a meal. It was the most wonderful-tasting frothy drink…much like the fresh fruit punch we'd had in the Caribbean in years past. Apparently it was guava mixed with milk, and prepared in a blender. I was rather anxious about the milk, but there were no side effects.

After dinner, Krys and I decided to sit on the outer rim of the grand hall and observe the other guests. Unfortunately, all of the ledges above had been selected by hundreds of pigeons as their night roosting place. They were flying about as well, and suddenly I heard Krys exclaim, "What was that?" Her nose, hair, even her dress, were all decorated with…you will know with what. A Rajasthani blessing, no doubt! We went to bed early, as the Maharajah himself had promised us a village safari, which would begin at 8:00 a.m. As he announced that he would be our personal guide, I noticed his quick, rather meaningful glance directed toward Miss Krystyna.

Saturday at the palace dawned with Krys announcing that she, who never succumbed to any sickness, had TD: traveler's diarrhea. In the night she had awakened with an explosive call to the loo and in the morning was feeling quite queasy. To go on the safari or not to go was the burning question. I had been feeling a bit iffy about setting out on yet another foray into the filth, stench, and scorching heat of the real India, but since we'd have to pay whether we went or not, we decided to give it a go. Our guide was, as I said before, a Maharajah. He was wearing a combination of Western wear and Rajasthani. He was very good-looking, with a small grey mustache and just a hint of the usual upward curl so familiar to his culture. We thought he was possibly about sixty-five, though without his hat, he looked older. He was wearing jeans, a striped shirt, American-style sunglasses, driving gloves and, can you believe it, a Tilly hat!

Krys and I sat in the front with him, and two Spanish girls from Madrid sat in the back of the Jeep. Since I was in the middle, I had to lean away from his hand as he changed gears. Mmm, was that planned? Your guess will be okay on that. More of this arrangement later! We drove through the city and were just beginning to see some of the sights on the outskirts when it began to rain--just a drizzle at first, but increasingly heavy as we went on. My thin cotton top was now sticking to my bra in a most suggestive manner and I was a bit concerned. However, I'm certain the Maharajah didn't mind. The safari consisted of numerous stops at villages where we, as guests of the Maharajah, were treated as honored visitors. We learned that he was a descendant of the famous Maharajah Pratap Singh, who was a very knowledgeable man and most intent on relaying all kinds of details and explanations of Rajathan's history and culture to his people.

When I asked if he had sons he replied, "We Rajathanis believe that all these people here in the villages are our sons." He gave us so much information that my head was swimming and I must admit that I couldn't recall all of it. Too bad, as most tourists don't get a chance to be treated to a tour with a real Maharajah! At the first village, he greeted the women and explained to us the meaning of their way of dressing--the significance of the nose jewelry, bracelets, ankle bracelets, and toe rings. Apparently, these are worn at pressure points in the body for good health. If you were a poor villager and could not afford a doctor as he could, you would wear a special silver bracelet to protect your health. The toe rings keep good fortune from escaping through the toes. The Maharajah's great wealth allows him to wear only string bracelets on his wrist pressure points and on his big toes to keep his wisdom from leaving his body. The Third Eye in the center of the forehead must be massaged every day to increase insight and wisdom. They cook in precious metal dishes, bowls, etc. to gain the vibrations from metal.

At village number two, we were again greeted respectfully and the Maharajah continued with a small lecture on spinning flax. He said that these lower-caste people have sunk to a lower level but have risen to a high level of craftsmanship. We saw blankets woven of camel hair, and ladies who were weaving a very coarse basic material. The ladies at the third village offered us a cup of tea. Uh-oh, I thought. What if they put milk in it before it's served? Krys assured me it would likely be black tea, but when a little boy served it, to my dismay, the milk was already in! Then to my delight, the Maharajah explained that there was no water in it--just boiled milk and tea. Beds were brought out, with soft green cushions on ours, and we took tea with the Maharajah of Jodhpur. The return trip reminded me a bit of my African safaris, as we saw gazelles making great leaps, water buffalo bathing, a mongoose, and some lizards--the oldest animals in the world, akin to dinosaurs.

The second safari trip began with a change in seating. Apparently one of the little Spanish girls was more than willing to sit next to him. I may have been imagining it, but I believe they had come to know each other quite well by now and she did not hesitate in taking the seat next to the gear shift! Krys sat next to her and I was relegated to the back seat with the other Spanish girl. That was fine with me, as he was too old for me. I preferred younger men even then. Oh, did I say that out loud? At each stop, Esther hurried to sit beside him, and we were soon to learn why. Esther (the little slut) had been on this same safari at least twice before. When she first took her place she sat with her legs apart so that the Maharajah would be required to reach between her legs to pull the clutch up! The symbolism was graphically clear, and I was not so naïve as to be mistaken in her desire to seduce

The Journey Itself

Swaroop Sing--a Maharajah who had descended from some very famous Maharajahs in Rajasthan.

As we drove along, she allowed her loose white blouse to blow in the wind and slip off her shoulder. She would pull it back in a halfhearted way in an attempt to cover her bare breasts. She was not wearing a bra, of course, but from what I could see from the back seat she didn't have much to be held in a bra. "Meow!" No matter, the Maharajah kept glancing down at her when she was most revealed. Obviously he was enjoying the show. When we stopped for tea at the next village, the Maharajah and Esther sat on chairs opposite his other clients, and we noticed him reading her palm. Even then I did not twig as to just how far things would go, but I was soon to find out. Esther put her hand on the Maharajah's leg, which he had left slack and adjacent to hers. She pressed with her fingers. I was certain she had selected one of those pressure points he'd told us about. You may recall his telling us about the Indian use of silver and gold. Esther already had the silver touch going for her, and I expected it would not be long before she moved on to the gold. She did not go as far as his crotch, though--perhaps because he was driving. That would have been too obvious. My surprise was that when we reached the hotel and exited the safari Jeep, Swaroop was able to stand without a revealing bulge in his jeans! The only other advance on our Maharajah's part was to grab her breast. He held his left arm down so that the breeze would blow his open shirt and screen what he was doing. I did not miss it, though. That night he declined our offer to dine with us. We assumed that he might need to be alone, either with his wife, with Esther, or with someone else.

The next day a special lunch had been prepared for us. We made pleasant conversation with Esther and Isobel. They were planning to see much more of India. Our Maharajah arrived just as we were completing lunch, and regaled us with many other stories of Rajasthan culture and history. One of the most blatant was that our eyes convey much more than our words ever could...as he fastened his eyes on Esther. Guess that's how men make passes in India, too.

When we were asked about our program, we were noncommittal and Isobel asked if she might join us. That left Esther with the Maharajah. From a distance we could hear him asking her the same question but could not hear her reply. So we will never know if she was successful in her seduction. However, when we returned she was seated outside the royal apartments, both in the afternoon and in the evening. We selected a table in the courtyard for dinner and were soon joined by Isobel and a young gentleman she had just met. Score two for the Spanish girls! Another couple were on their way to Jaisalmer. I argued with myself about describing it, but only mentioned the flies and really understated what I had said to myself when I was there: "Please God, get me out of this hellhole!"

Krys and I decided to try the Trio Restaurant, which had been recommended by another traveller. It must have been a person who wished us ill, for the table was covered with black flies even before our order arrived. Despite this, I tried the club sandwich and some hard boiled eggs, plus yogurt. It was a tough battle, but I managed to get the food in my mouth as I swished the flies away. When we returned to our hotel, I announced that I should take my malaria pill. Krys thought I should skip it as every time I took my weekly pill there were serious side effects. It was the first trip for which the travel clinic in Toronto had recommended Chloroquin, so I apparently did not suspect it for the weekly distress I had felt a number of times prior to this.

It began after Krys and I had enjoyed our candlelight and incense reverie in our hotel room. We had packed for an early departure from the Ajet Bahwan Hotel and our transfer to the

Umaid Bahwan. We decided to go to bed a bit early, and then my worst assault began. I had felt a bit dizzy at dinner but had ascribed it to the heat and the candlelight. My legs and arms were all a-tingle, right down to my fingers and toes. My brain had a strange numbed sensation. It seemed like some of my reactions to antihistamines and codeine. Krys had fallen asleep and I didn't want to bother her, so I went into the bathroom and sat in a tub of cool water. I was so hot that I gained some relief which did not last. The sensations were so alarming that I repeated "the water treatment." Next I tried sitting in a chair with a wet washcloth on my forehead and over my eyes. I was desperately thirsty, so I took glass after glass of water (supposedly safe to drink). Krys woke up and was really surprised to see me sitting in the chair. I told her I felt like someone on drugs who is experiencing a really bad trip! Krys knew of nothing that would help and said she guessed I'd just have to sit out the night. I hunted up the sheet which the doctor had given me-- the one about side effects from Chloroquin. I had all of them! As Krys and I reminisced about the other times I had experienced similar symptoms, we realized that Barb should never again take said pill! Finally after three or four hours I was able to sit up in bed, and "the night from hell" was over.

Fortunately we were already packed so we went out for breakfast and to check out. As usual, the table was covered with flies and, although I wasn't hungry, I did have a cup of tea. Not an easy thing to do. Put your hand over the cup, take a sip, then cover it again. I thought but did not utter aloud, God I hate flies; I hate the heat, the dirt and, yes, I'm soon going to write I hate India! Come now, Barb, did you ever think you'd say you hate your beloved India? I supposed that this one incident would not allow me to do that. Surely I could never bring myself to say this. Perhaps when I was back home, the memories of untoward events and all negative aspects of my other three trips to India would be forgotten. I would recall the emotions when I first saw the Taj Mahal, Jaipur's Amber Palace, the home stays with the millionaires, and my wonderful experiences in Kashmir.

The motorized rickshaw mini cab driver had been waiting for us for at least an hour and a half and agreed to a 20 ra fare from the hotel and back. When he saw the two big packages, I would expect him to think we had enough money to give him more. Plus we were staying in a huge four or five star hotel. When Krys was paying him, she asked how much it would be. He asked for 1000 to 5000 ra, so Krys entered into the usual bargaining mode. "But we have no big boxes, just lots of paper." The settled amount was 2000 ra.

When we returned to our hotel I lay down for a while and Krys checked out the Umaid Bahwan museum. After that it was time for dinner. I enjoyed a chicken stroganoff and chocolate ice cream sundae. It was great to have real food again, and no flies! We went to bed early so we could get up by 6:30 a.m. We intended to get some good pictures of our Mausoleum/Palace/Hotel before we left. The hotel was so wide that we were not able to get far enough away to take a good picture, so we took it in sections. Now that the Jodhpur part of our tip was over, it was back to Delhi and on to our flight home.

Krys talked sweetly to management, saying that since we had stayed at the Imperial Hotel three times, we felt a deluxe room would be very nice. He readily agreed and we were shown to a superb accommodation. The following day was to be a visit to Fort Gulab, leaving at 8:45 a.m. Our guide arrived right on time. He really was a sweet man and Krys insisted that she thought he was sweet on me. He asked to have his picture taken with me--or as he said, "Mommie Barbara." I didn't believe I would ever write to him, but we exchanged business cards anyway.

The Journey Itself

August 26 was our last day in India. I hate to admit it but I thanked God that I was going home to Brechinbrae, my lovely home in the hills of Medonte. No more worries about clean water and edible food. The next day we rose early so we could go to India Travel to collect our refund--$187 US. It took a long time--two or three hours...typical Indian service, particularly anything to do with money! However, we were suitably rewarded for our trouble. Not only did we get the unused flight amount, but some off on hotels as well. Krys and I felt like millionaires with our thousands of rupees--actually only $187 US, but a lot of paper. Naturally we felt compelled to spend it, and we had only two hours to accomplish that. We hired a taxi and were off to an emporium. Our driver was a Sikh with a huge pink turban and terrible teeth--only a few ,with huge, ugly spaces above and below. However, he was really good-natured and willing to wait for three hours if necessary. "No problem, Madam; I will wait." I recalled the many times I had heard, "No problem" while in India.

Our driver then took us to the Taj Hotel, where I bought a wonderful black silk outfit: pants, long tunic top, and shawl. I likely won't wear it at home, but one never knows. I already had two Indian sarees that didn't get much use. We went up to the rooftop restaurant to check out the menu. I recalled a superb French restaurant from another trip, but it was now Italian. The menu looked great and, since we were now wealthy, the prices seemed a great bargain. Krys said we should have champagne, but at over 4000 rupees per bottle, even the "nouveau riche" duo considered it too expensive. Krys had decided to buy another black studded Michael Jackson jacket. This required a visit to the Sheraton Hotel, so we slipped in there to the shop we had visited the first night, when we had had dinner there. Of course they had another jacket. No problem!

Camel Safari in Rajasthan

My first trip to the Taj Hotel had blown me away--and this time some things were familiar; others not. One could never forget the amazing lobby, with white marble everywhere, beautiful bouquets of flowers, and ornate vaulted ceilings of bright red, blue, purple, and gold. I remembered my stay here ten years prior to this when John Heeg and Josephine accompanied me to the wonderful sound and light show at the Red Fort. Ricky, the Sikh guide, had been happy to take us there and to receive his sizable tip. Even the huge vases of amazing white jasmine flowers were the same.

Next we decided to sort our money to pay bills we knew were coming up. A certain number of rupees would be required for the departure tax, cab to the airport, and to clear our hotel bill. Krys was in charge of that. Then each of us would have a stash to be "wasted." Naturally we headed for the emporium, where a certain wildness overtook us. After all, if we spent all our rupees we could resort to credit cards. Ah yes, the amazing invention of credit cards! It wasn't long before I heard Krys call out, "Barb, I've spent all our dinner money and cab fares!" So it would be credit cards after all.

At 6:30 p.m. the moment of truth had come--the final packing! All went quite well, though you will be surprised to learn what we had to squeeze into our bags. My large Concord suitcase was fortunately expandable, and Krys had a very large case as well. Plus I had my huge Ecuador backpack. The contents of the suitcases, as well as our clothes, included an incense burner, Jaisalmer tablecloths x 3, a bedspread, 17 cushion covers with camels and elephants on them, and the famously packed boxes from Jodhpur. We were actually able to assign them to our suitcases. We would take my video camera and other necessities in our carry-ons.

The Journey Itself

We called a cab at 8:00 p.m. and headed for the elegant Taj hotel--the Italian restaurant in particular. The driver said he'd wait for us. Rather nice to have our very own driver just hanging about at our beck and call. He insisted that he would also take us to the airport at midnight. Our dinner was magnificent: Italian white wine, fresh salad with artichoke, huge prawns with vegetables, and a light pasta in a delicate tomato sauce. They didn't have cappuccino, so we ordered regular coffee and an intriguing dessert--like éclairs, with chocolate sauce and cream. Mmm! At dinner, one of the hostesses spoke to us briefly at first, then returned to talk in depth. She regretted that we were leaving that night, as she was very interested in America, particularly Canada. She was quite beautiful, with eyes that reminded me of the classic Indian Maharani depicted in Rajasthani paintings. Further conversation revealed that her father was a hotel owner, that she had been raised in Pampa (Himachel Prudish) and that she knew the Dalai Lama quite well. We spoke of the picture that had been taken of Krys and me with His Holiness, and she was surprised that he had allowed that private audience.

On August 27 we left for Indira Gandhi International Airport. At one check point our driver announced, "International Airport." We were passed through easily. The traffic was unreal --all jammed up with trucks and cars, but our driver broke through and we were off to the airport undeterred. Our flight was delayed until 4:00 a.m., so the hurry to be there at midnight was all for naught. Our flight arrived at Heathrow, where Krys and I would go to her aunt's for one night and I would leave the next day for the airport, to fly to Paris for an overnight at the Sofitel Hotel. My checked luggage had been assigned to go right on to Toronto when we left India. Aunt Jola gave us tea, cheese, and some plum sweets. Very nice. She mentioned that the weather had been unusually cool for the past three weeks. However, I never thought I'd welcome cool weather with such enthusiasm. India's heat in August's monsoon season is horrible!

August 28, 10:07 a.m. and I was back at the Charles de Gaulle Airport, awaiting my last flight. I was so glad to be going home. Really glad! This, perhaps, had been my most difficult trip of all! I was sick three or four times--desperately sick twice. And the different legs of the trip each required a difficult adjustment for me. I would not miss the awful heat, dirty streets, mediocre accommodation, flies, and the Indian food. Krys did not like to hear me say that I might never return to India and had a long list of rationalizations meant to dissuade me of that. My transfer to the airport was easy and I checked in at 9:30 p.m. I was pleased to get a bulkhead, but went further, on my pilot son's suggestion. However, an upgrade to first class was not in the cards for me that night. Have I forgotten to tell you about the ridiculously high prices at the Sofitel? A tiny meal the night before (one beer, one soup, one roll, and a small dish of chocolate ice cream), plus a continental breakfast: (one juice, one coffee, two rolls)--$ 68.00 US!

My flight home was aboard Air France. I had a very comfortable seat, bulkhead, with an aisle seat, and I was heading for home! A few drinks of Scotch plus a pleasant dinner, and I was able to sit back and relax. We expected to land at 2:20 p.m. and I was hoping Morley would not have had to wait too long. It was always the long-suffering Morley who greeted me. What a guy! People always asked if he ever went with me. Of course a farmer's work is never done. With 55 head of cattle, haying and threshing, plus his real estate, he could not get away often. We did go on some cruises in the winter, but I was always teaching then and I had to choose my summer holidays to do most of my travelling.

Circumnavigating the World

In 1998, out of the blue, a fascinating trip presented itself to me. It was named "Circumnavigating the World" and we would be at sea for four months. You heard me correctly, I said, "four months." At this point my travel diary would have suggested that I might have already seen most of the world. However, that would not be totally accurate. There were many destinations still on my bucket list, and the ones I'd already visited were worthy of revisiting--hence the decision to give it a go. The sailing was scheduled for the year 2000, so it could be my project for the turn of the century.

Part of my pre-trip planning included a trip to Toronto. I had an idea to propose to the travel company--one that I hoped might reduce the cost of my trip. Since I had been on 30 trips of my own and had slide presentations for most of them, I wondered if the company might like to have me present some of these. As a matter of fact, I had one slide presentation that included all seven continents, and this world tour would include photos from each continent we would visit. They were polite and listened to my proposal, but, in the end, declined my offer.

Four months is a long time to be on a ship, but I pictured myself writing the novel that I had been researching and writing for about eight years. The Diaz Crystal was historical fiction with parts of fantasy. It involved the fall of the Inca Empire when Francisco Pizarro and his band of only 200 conquistadors conquered over 10,000 Inca. The fantasy part involved time travel for the heroine of the book. At one point she travels back in time to become the Inca king's favorite concubine. Of course I would need a laptop computer, so that was one of my many pre-trip purchases. Another was the need to acquire new camera equipment. I always took hundreds of slides on every one of my many trips.

Since we were sailing from Aeneas, in Greece, I booked the Atlantica Aeneas Hotel near the port. An overnight stay would have me there, ready to embark the following day. As well, I had enough points for my flight, so I took care of that also. With those bases covered, I felt really good about the forthcoming adventure.

Prior to each trip I regularly went to the Toronto General Hospital. They had a travel clinic where I could receive injections or pills for the numerous exotic places I would visit. With that checked off my list I could concentrate on my wardrobe for the various climates we would encounter. People always agree that preparing for a trip and looking forward to it are some of the best parts of travelling. That's true for me as well. I had travelled with this particular company twice in my recent past so, when they asked if I would act as a reference resource for them, I was quite pleased to do so. I even had one telephone call from Tel Aviv!

About two weeks before we would embark on this marvelous cruise, I had an e-mail from the company's office in Toronto. "Sorry to inform you but the place of departure will be Spain, not Greece. More info will follow." My heart sank. The hotel would need to be canceled as well as the flight, and I didn't even have a new date of departure. I will spare you the expletives, as that would not be

The Journey Itself

ladylike. However, I must confess to some of my less-obnoxious thoughts. Having my own travel company allowed me to consider that it would not be unusual for certain complications to arise, particularly for a trip that would be four months long. Not to worry, I mused. Things will go all right in the end.

About a week before we would begin this cruise, I received yet another e-mail. The ship would also be changed from a chartered 800-passenger vessel to the chartered Riviera which held about 400 passengers. The company was going to book a hotel for everyone and pay not only for the accommodation, but also the meals while we were there. They did not know how long that would be as this new ship had to be prepared for sailing. Alarm bells went off when I heard that part. The ship had to be prepared to sail! What kind of cruise ship is not immediately ready to sail? I asked myself what was really going on--even considered canceling, but they had my money... make that a whole lot of money...and I more or less had to go. I don't believe you can collect insurance for backing out unless the insurance company would consider hysteria as a medical reason for changing one's mind. Actually, I had suffered worse disappointments on my previous 29 trips. This could still be the adventure of a lifetime, and I planned to make it just that.

Once I had the date of departure, I was able to make the flight reservation and Air Canada was willing to transfer my original points payment to the rearranged flight. I was travelling alone, so I wasn't sharing a cabin. As far as I knew, no one from Ontario was even going on this world cruise. I had been contacted by a gentleman who had been on the first world cruise with this company. Their circumnavigation had been further south than the one I chose, and he wished me well. He just hoped I would not be on the same ship as their cruise. Well, I thought, at least we will have a better ship as they are waiting for a new one. Forget that. Did they not say they were preparing said ship?

Circumnavigating the World

When I arrived in Madrid and checked in at the hotel, many passengers were already there, as was a representative for the Toronto company. I felt sorry for him as he was being bombarded by questions he couldn't answer and complaints about things that weren't his fault. However, by dinner time, things had settled down and most seemed to be optimistic. I sat at a table for ten and soon was making friends with some of my mates who would be onboard the Riviera. One generous fellow even told me he was "available"! I named him "Available Ed." Another guy from Texas introduced himself as Loyd (with one L). Loyd would become very helpful in the near future.

Each morning, when we went into the lobby, the bulletin board read, "No date of departure yet." Now the previously irritated guests began to grow even more restless, and more annoyed. Some were a family of four or five, with two or three children to amuse. They would have spent much more than $30,000 US. I saw them harassing the company's frustrated agent, all to no avail. He did not have answers for them and he was in no way accountable. One good thing was that we were getting splendid meals, and the company was paying for everything.

Finally, on the fifth day the bulletin board had good news. We were departing the next day for Seville. The large luggage would be taken by truck, so we were asked to leave it outside our room door by 7:00 a.m. We would be transported to the train station, after breakfast, which was to be at 8:00 a.m. This was both good news and bad news for me. If you will recall, I would have laptop, camera equipment, and backpack to deal with as I got on the bus; then, at the train station, I would have to walk to my assigned train car to board, loaded with all of my stuff Hey, who ever said travelling is easy? Not me, anyway, though I continue to do it despite the fact that in the year 2000 I was 70 years old! Still no pity from my reader? Okay, I was getting what I deserved. However, I must tell you that this was the first of many times that Loyd with one L came to help me with all of the carry-ons.

There was to be an overnight in Seville; then it would be on to the Port of Cadiz. At the hotel in Seville, my bedroom was up a very high flight of stairs, so I contacted the desk and demanded something better. Yes, I pulled the old age card and my serious arthritis. The following morning we all climbed aboard the bus and we were off to Cadiz. Some of the travelers were placing bets as to whether there would actually be a ship there. I didn't think this was in the least amusing as, after all we'd been through, no ship would mean no world cruise, and the company would have our money!

As we neared the port we were able to see that there was a ship. Notice that I did not say, "a lovely ship" or "a great ship." My reason for this is that it looked like a very old ship, probably dragged out of dry dock. The lecture staff was manning fork lifts as they loaded everything onto the ship. Did this mean there wasn't much of a crew? The cabins were not ready. There was no bedding, no shower curtain, soap, or towels--only a small bouquet of flowers on an otherwise bare side table. This cabin was like no other I had previously been assigned to on the more than twelve other cruises I had experienced. We did have a wonderful dinner, and people were chatting and getting to know one another. One elderly gentleman, who was seated at my table, declared that his only reason for choosing this trip was because it would take us to Pitcairn Island. My disappointment was that Barb would not be sitting on deck tapping out the rest of her novel on her laptop. The reason being that, unlike your usual cruise ship, this old ship didn't actually have a proper deck, with chairs and all!

Since I'm the proverbial optimist, I still held out hope that the ports of call would make up for the other disappointments. Who would not want to visit Morocco, Italy, Spain, Antarctica, the Mayan and Incan ruins, Panama, Ecuador, Peru, Chile, Pitcairn, Western Samoa, the Solomon Islands, Papua New Guinea, Vietnam, Singapore, Thailand, India, the Seychelles, Kenya, Djibouti, Jordan, Egypt, and Israel? I have left out some of the destinations, as I believe you may be getting rather bored with my litany of places we were supposed to see. They were all identified and meticulously described, as to history and points of interest, in a beautifully bound book entitled Lost Worlds—A Guide to the Places We Visit.

When my cabin was finally set up properly, I was prepared to be content, and things went rather well. The other travelers were interesting and quite amiable. "Available Ed" was doing his best to win me over, though I was determined that he would not succeed in a final coup! And Loyd was helpful in other ways that did not include a possibility of intimacy. The bathroom was tiny and access was gained by navigating up a rather high step. The going up was manageable, but one had to be cautious stepping back down into the cabin, particularly if there was any roll to the ship. Things went well for the first three days. After all, we were still in the Mediterranean Sea. However, on the fourth morning, I grew careless and, as I stepped down from the bathroom into the cabin, I felt myself falling and reached back with my right arm to grab the doorway. Big mistake! Prior to the cruise, I had been seeing a physiotherapist for a rotator cuff problem. So that shoulder was vulnerable and I had a great deal of pain. I phoned the ship's doctor, but he was unable to see me. He was trying to save a dying man's life. Okay, I suppose that poor patient outranked me in the priority category. I'd have to wait.

Later that day, the doctor examined me and thought nothing was broken. He put my arm in a sling and said we were scheduled to land at a small island in two days. If nothing was broken, I would be fine to continue. He still didn't have any insurance papers for me to fill out, but he was certain he'd have them soon. I was a bit concerned, but still optimistic. The X-ray at the clinic showed that nothing was broken and, when I spoke to the chief administrator aboard the ship, she advised that there would be no reason to "abandon ship" (my words) and discontinue the world cruise. With my retired teachers' insurance, one must advise their office, within 48 hours, of any medical event. I did so right there in the administrator's office and was minimally satisfied that I'd be all right with my insurance. But--and that's a serious "but"--with no receipts from the doctor I'd be out of luck when I got home. As a precautionary move, I happened to be seated next to the doctor's wife at dinner that night and asked for their US address and phone number. As a last resort I'd be able to contact him after the trip.

The first major destination was Morocco and I was excited about that, as it was still on my bucket list. The cruise planners had also affirmed that, if one wished to extend time at a destination, provision was made to rejoin the cruise ship later on. I had no idea how that would happen, but assumed that arrangements had been made by the company.

My shoulder was still seriously hurting and, now that my arm was in a sling, everything I did was a problem. I gave slight consideration to throwing in the towel, but hated to give up. Two years of planning and organizing to be away from home for four months had taken a great deal of my time; I had looked forward to this cruise being the trip of a lifetime and a great number of the destinations intrigued me. Was I about to "wimp out" now? I didn't have a dream, nor do I claim to be psychic, but when I awoke several days later, I had a gut feeling that Barb should plan to go home. When I spoke to the main administrator again, she said, "If nothing is broken, I think you should stay."

However, my mind was made up and steps were arranged for my departure. A port agent came on board to reserve a hotel in Madeira for one night, to hire a taxi to take me to the hotel and to the airport the following day. Lastly he would make the final plane reservations: Madeira to New York and a second one for New York to Toronto. All of this was paid with my MasterCard. So it was Barb, all alone with all of her baggage, heading home…not quite all of my baggage, though, as the port agent had arranged for the heavy bags to be delivered to the New York airport.

I distinctly remember how arduous it was to repack everything. My toiletries were in the bathroom and all of my clothes for four months were on the unused bunk across from mine. I can still see myself, with my arm in a sling, crawling across the cabin floor to pack the big suitcase and the backpack. Then I had to pull out the laptop from under my bunk and arrange all my camera equipment to fill my camera bag.

The taxi driver delivered me to Casino Park Resort Hotel and I settled in for my very brief stay. My view of this lovely little Portuguese island of Madeira might inspire me to return someday when I could stay much longer. After dinner, I called my pilot son, John, to see if he could meet me in Toronto. He was available, so I gave him the flight number and expected time of arrival from New York. As we spoke, he said that his brother's divorce was not going well, so I called Roy as well. I left a message on his answering machine that he was not to worry, as Mom was coming home.

The hotel gave me an early wake-up call and arranged for a taxi to the airport. I was in lots of time for my flight. Harried, but more or less confident that I "had it together", I sat in the departure lounge wondering what else might go wrong. The flight left on time and, by then, my baggage was stored and all my carry-on was looked after by a most efficient flight attendant.

The Journey Itself

New York was another challenge. Before we landed, I advised the attendant that I would need a wheelchair, not so much for the walking, but so we could pile the carry-ons around me as I was seated. At the New York airport the girl assigned to me was a very proficient African-American. When I gave her the number of my boarding lounge, she told me it had been changed. However, we would first have to go to identify my checked luggage and take it to the check-in counter. Nothing seemed to bother this amazing lady. She selected a cart for my luggage, pushed my wheelchair and pulled the cart. We finally arrived at the correct departure lounge and I was left with all my "stuff." Unfortunately, a guy came along and took my wheelchair. I hoped that someone would help me when it was time to board.

Good luck on that, Barb. Long before we would board, an attendant came to take all of the rest of the travelers to another lounge. This left me alone, with no wheelchair and no one to carry my laptop, camera equipment, and backpack. When I spoke to the desk attendant his answer was that all would be well. Remember, I was the sole passenger left in that lounge; I don't know where the others were, and the guy on the desk was blissfully unconcerned!

When time to board drew near, I returned to the desk and announced, "If you won't help me I will have to drag all this stuff, piece by piece, to wherever my fellow passengers have been taken!" He finally gave in, and away we went. All of the others had already boarded, and the gal at the gate was urging me to make haste. She carried my bags and on I went…just in time. Some entity must be looking out for me, I mused.

A few days after my return to my home at Brechinbrae, I began the troublesome job of applying for my insurance. One would think that it would just be a matter of submitting the appropriate forms to the insurance company. Wrong! It seems that the company's employees are dedicated to paying as little as possible. Each submission resulted in another letter that consistently contained the same quote, "We have received your application but, if we just had . . . . , we could settle your request." Fortunately, I had kept every receipt, every credit card stub with my signature, the doctor's report complete with his signature, etc. Finally, after many back and forth communications and about a month of negotiating, a Fed Ex representative arrived at my door with a check, and all was settled to my satisfaction.

What happened to my fellow passengers? Well, I must state here that my decision to "jump ship" was a really good choice. About a month after I left, I had an e-mail from Loyd (with one L). A week or so before they arrived at Tahiti, the passengers were required to pay for their meals. Then, the travelers were notified that the following day they would be disembarking. The company said they would see that they got to the airport. However, the e-mails I received from Ed and Loyd suggested that it was "every man for himself," with no help from the cruise company.

We learned later that only one third of the circumnavigation was completed and the company had gone broke. A local newspaper report declared that a round-the-world cruise, which left Spain in April, was cut short in Tahiti. It stated that the high cost of fuel was the main reason. However, I had my own assumptions. The first world cruise was able to complete the entire trip, as our payments for the second cruise would allow that to happen. More bad news arrived by e-mail from my friends Ed and Loyd. Ed had paid with a credit card, so he was okay with his claim. However, Loyd had not paid with a card and he was totally out of luck. Too bad, as he was a really nice guy.

My summation for this story must be that you not plan to go on a cruise that sounds too good to be true, because this one was definitely a disaster! Recently, I gleaned more information from

The Journey Itself

the internet. Christopher Reynolds, a travel writer for Travel Insider, posted an item on June 4, 2000. Permit me to quote Christopher with the following: "Six words you don't want to hear from a person in authority in the middle of an around-the-world cruise: I have bad news for you. But that's what a ship official told passengers on the cruise ship Riviera on the morning of May 23, those passengers recall. The ship was just docking in Papeete, Tahiti. Fresh from breakfast, about 200 passengers were summoned to the ship's lounge. The company had run out of money, the official told them. World Cruise Co. and the cruise operator, would cease operations, and a trustee would oversee the company's dissolution. Instead of sailing on to the Solomon Islands, passengers would disembark that day. Those passengers had counted on World Cruise Co. to take them around the world in 116 days. Most paid more than $14,000, including shore excursions and extras and boarded the Riviera in Cadiz, Spain on April 13. On day 41, those plans collapsed. Passengers and ship's personnel tried to find flights home and figure out who would pay for them. Though passengers were initially told that World Cruise Co. would cover their air fares home, five passengers said they ended up paying their own way."

Christopher Reynolds - Times Travel Writer
for TRAVEL INSIDER

I had a number of e-mails from some of the other passengers I had met while onboard the Riviera. They confirmed that they were "in the same boat". What I am trying to say is that, as far as I know, none of the passengers received their return airfare, let alone any refund for the 76 days remaining in their circumnavigation of the world. In the end, I believe the reader will agree that I made the correct decision to return home.

It took a while to receive satisfactory compensation from my insurance company. Many letters, requesting just one more document to prove my reason for leaving the cruise, were required but in the end I was satisfied. I was home receiving my insurance check while the Riviera was making its way to Tahiti and the unpropitious end of the world cruise!

CPSIA information can be obtained
at www.ICGtesting.com
Printed in the USA
BVOW06s0145111116
467348BV00002B/23/P

9 781478 701606